THE BOOK OF WINE

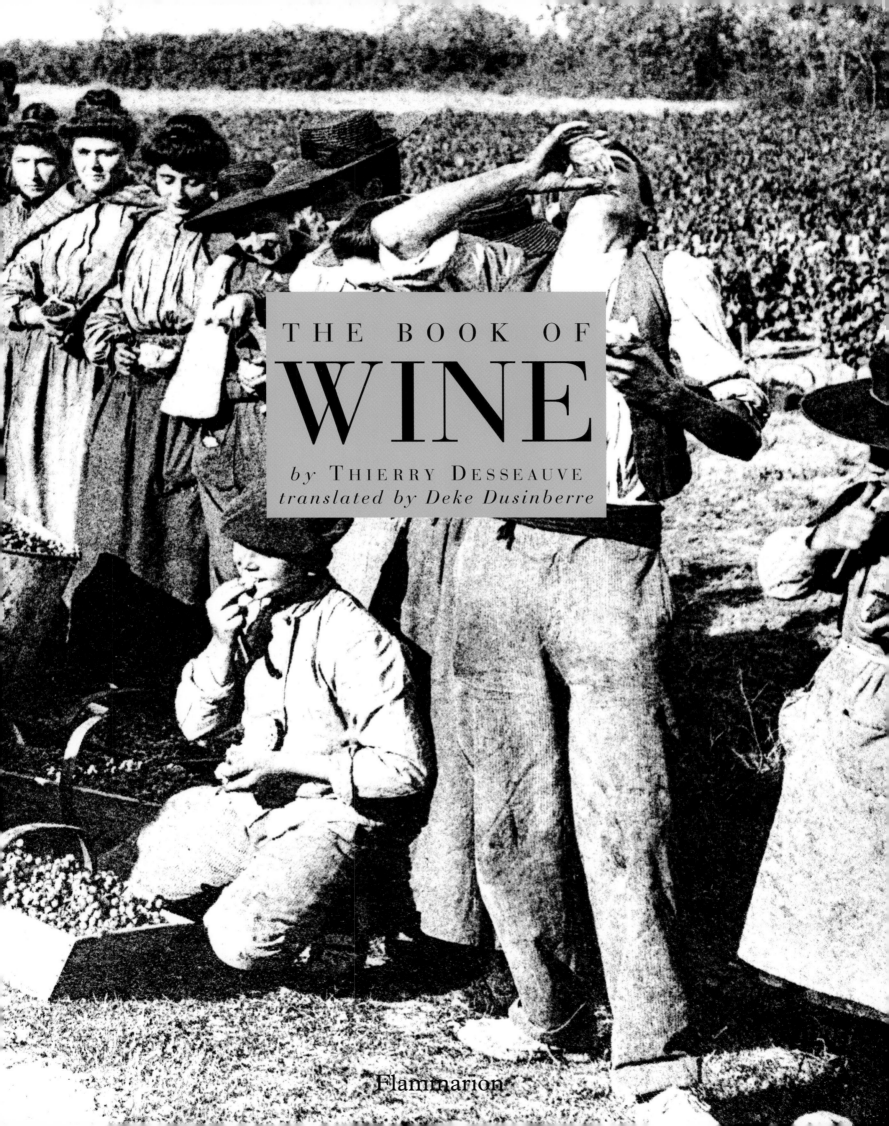

THE BOOK OF
WINE

by THIERRY DESSEAUVE
translated by Deke Dusinberre

Flammarion

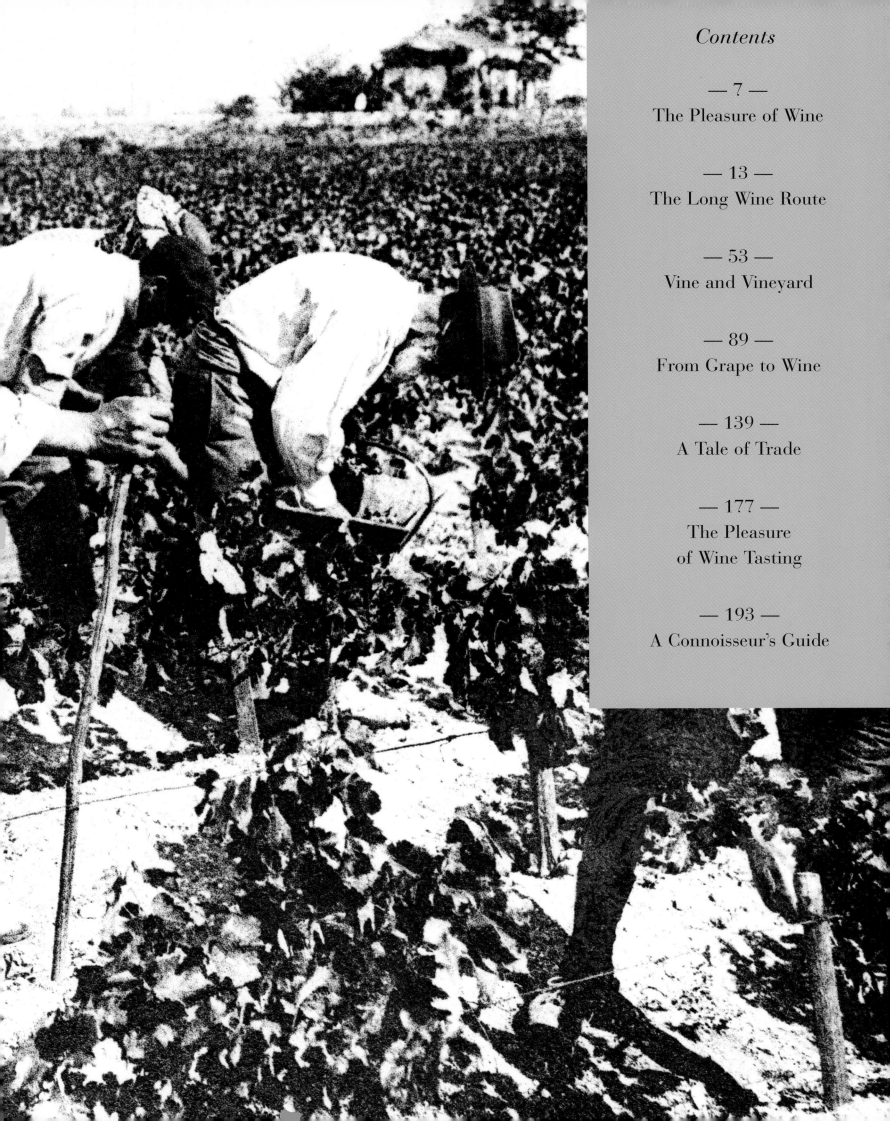

Contents

The Pleasure of Wine

A walnut—
What's inside a walnut?
What do you see
When it's shut?
You see the night so round
with its hills and its downs,
all its rivers, valleys and mounds.

A walnut—
What's inside a walnut?
What do you see
Once it's open?
There's no time to look:
You munch and you kiss
—no time to sigh—
you just munch and you kiss
discoveries goodbye.

Please forgive me for beginning this book with a regret, but it does seem a shame that the muse handed French crooner Charles Trenet a walnut rather than glass of wine. By "glass" I am not referring to those simple vessels praised by the bards of alcohol and dingy bistros, but rather to a fine stemmed glass, round and curvaceous, filled two-thirds full with a flaming purple-red wine, a bold robust wine from Roussillon, Narbonne, or Pézenas. Just think what Trenet would have seen there, in the reflections of that nectar, in the lively hues of its color!

The color of a wine reflects the centuries that have shaped its sloping vineyard, the labor of growers, and the sun that has ripened the grapes. The color of a wine conveys its vigor and concentration when the hue is brilliant and opaque; it reveals its age when the edges along the side of the glass take on golden highlights. And it also reflects the eagerness of assembled guests and the pleasure that lies in store for them.

This is were we part paths with Trenet. Because once you taste a wine, the discoveries have only just begun. An entire chapter of this book would not suffice to list the all fragrances detected by a connoisseur's sharp senses, to describe all the multifarious comparisons that the human nose can draw from the organoleptic subtleties of a vintage. The aromas that exalt a youthful vintage, for instance, include the cedar and tobacco of great red wines from Médoc and Napa Valley, the rose and lichee of a Gewürztraminer, the flinty scent of a Chablis, the walnut—naturally!—of an Andalusian sherry, the raisin of Sicilian Marsala, or the blackcurrant and blackberry of Hermitage wines from the Rhône Valley. Later, after sheltering for a few years in the gloom of a cellar, a wine will deliver new nuances and new scents intricately woven into a complex ensemble that an imaginative winemaker one day handsomely named "bouquet."

"O profound joys of wine, who has never known you? All who have ever had remorse to drown, memories to stir, a sorrow to allay, or a castle in the air to build, all have invoked you, O mysterious god hidden in the fibers of the vine. How grand are wine's spectacles, illumined by an inner sun! How true and burning is this second youth that man draws from it! Yet how dreadful also are its explosive sensuality and its exasperating enchantment."

One of the ways to contain the explosion of exasperation and sensuality proved by the enchantments described by Baudelaire in *Du vin et du Haschich* is perhaps to remain both demanding and moderate in one's pleasures, preferring a single glass of a great vintage to ten bottles of ordinary wine!

Yet all these sights and smells are mere preliminaries to the final stage of pleasure—it is important to take things nice and slow—which comes when at last the wine is in the mouth. A mouthful of the selected, noble grapes that go into the mellowest Alsatian wines will line the palate indefinitely, while a measure of Pouilly Fumé sharply awakens the taste buds. Some wines, when savored for a few seconds before being swallowed, evoke geometric shapes: square for a Pauillac; square, too, but with rounder edges, for a Saint-Emilion; spherical for a Volnay, and so on. Other, less successful, wines are less ordered: the strength of the alcohol might provide an initial jolt, then the wine tumbles, finishing thin and unremarkable in the throat. For in the end it is swallowed, this precious mouthful, to be remembered for a long time to come.

When the wine is good, that is. There is no point in discussing wines whose only spirit is their 12.5% alcoholic content and whose place of origin is best identified by the bottling company's zip code. Only great wines spark passion and curiosity. For centuries now, the craft of winemaking has drawn mankind, earth and sky together, each contributing its nature, its talent or its changeability to induce vines to bear ripe, generous grapes that will in turn yield a nectar with highlight of gold or deepest red. Great wines can be dazzling. They may lead to drunkenness, but only in the sense that Baudelaire used the term: "You must be drunk at all times. That's the nub of it, the sole issue. In order not to feel the burden of Time that weighs on your shoulders and presses you toward the ground, you must be drunk without reprieve. But on what? On wine, poetry or virtue, as you like. But get drunk."

This type of drunkenness comes from wine—from its history, its geography, its makers, and its special ambiance. It can suddenly overtake you at the bend of a path, in a cellar, or in the back of a wine store. For myself, this drunkenness occurred during one of those vineyard tours methodically and enthusiastically undertaken by every self-respecting wine lover. The great moment might have happened in Bordeaux, California, or Tuscany, but in fact it occured at Châteauneuf-du-Pape, near Avignon.

It is hard to imagine a vineyard with more mystique than Château Rayas, which produces a very small quantity of red wine of astonishing finesse and depth, snapped up by wealthy and patient connoisseurs the world over. Whereas most Châteauneuf-du-Pape reds are powerful, almost heavy wines made for boisterous hunting banquets featuring hearty dishes of game in sauce, Rayas startles by its aristocratic reserve, and by its body which at first diffident but finally lines the palate, leaving in the mouth a lingering of its aromatic complexity. The lucky few with the good fortune to have tasted this red wine can only hope to stumble one day across its white counterpart, which is even more elusive. And even if you try to decipher the enigma on the spot, the mystery remains.

Château Rayas takes a mischievous delight in remaining impossible to find from both far and near: no road signs, not even a paved road to reach the winery, no external indication to tell pilgrims that they have finally

Two examples of unforgettable wines: Château Gruaud-Larouse (*above*) and Château Rayas (*right*, displayed by wine merchant Marc Sibard at Caves Augé in Paris). Gruaud-Larouse, whose label proudly proclaims it "The king of wines, the wine of kings," is one of the most famous Saint-Julien vineyards. Like many other prestigious estates in Bordeaux, it has had many different owners. In the past ten years alone ownership has shifted from the Cordier wine firm to the Alcatel industrial corporation and then back into the fold of a Bordeaux merchant, the Taillan company. Fortunately, however, the quality of the wine has held steady, thanks to the technical staff which has remained the same. From this standpoint, the life of a great Châteauneuf-du-Pape vineyard such as Château Rayas has been far calmer—the estate has belonged to the Reynaud family since 1890.

reached their destination. And even once the holy of holies has been reached, this quest for the grail may take another surprising turn. The winery is housed in a simple Provençal farmhouse of no particular charm, flanked by a coarse concrete terrace where the grapes are brought during harvesting.

This is where the pilgrim may have encountered the master of the premises, Jacques Reynaud, a small, lean man whose face nevertheless retained a strangely child-like expression. And that is where a curious entrance exam took place, on the doorstep, in the course of erratic conversation in which Reynaud ran through the one's religious beliefs or interest in the institution of the monarchy. The conversation, intercut with long silences that seemed to embarrass only the visitor, might have gone on for twenty or thirty minutes, until Reynaud decided either to abandon the pilgrim, lost in the middle of nowhere, or on the contrary to invite him into the winery. A few cement vats from another era, a floor of packed earth, colorless walls, old steps and dark corridors led at last to a few rows of ancient casks and barrels. At this point the examination continued as Reynaud rummaged for his pipette and two glasses of doubtful cleanliness. Woe to the amateur taster who might wax ecstatic over the first wine offered, usually taken from a cask that the owner intended to eliminate from the final blend. Only if this last of countless pitfalls was avoided would the wonderful wines finally arrive, all different according to whether they came from older or younger vines, from brighter or duller soil, yet all forcefully recalling the vineyard's forthright elegance. With consummate and ruthless artistry, Reynaud would select the few casks worthy of composing the final blend of the Rayas vintage. The pilgrim emerged from his visit happy and disoriented, in another world outside time, drunk on mixed emotions.

Jacques Reynaud departed for the great vineyard in the sky a few years ago, but Château Rayas remains a living paradox, at the extremes of technical and human canons now applied to wines, both locally and worldwide. But this living contradiction is also a brilliant demonstration. Although winemaking—like the movies—has become an industry, the creative process behind a high quality wine is still rooted in a multitude of traditional factors, all of them interlinked in constantly varying ways and proportions.

Motives, history, traditions, periods, attitudes, talent—all these and more go to make wine much more than a food product, more than an agrochemical process, more than a drink that gives a serious hangover to anyone who overdoes it. Great wine requires explanation, study, assessment. Yet beyond such Cartesian rationalism, a great wine also offers subtle aromas that are pure magic, profound flavors so full of spirit and imagination that they confound all the most pompous professors. This book is therefore designed to respect wine's generous, imaginative impulse by constantly leavening explanation with anecdote. Each section of the various chapters of this book focuses on an example or incident arising from travels or encounters, making it easier to grasp the importance of a given aspect or feature. Rather than propose yet another theoretical treatise on wine, it seemed preferable to explain things through illustration and example. So as this book flows from anecdote to history down the long river of wine, it hopes to initiate readers into the delightful paradox that great wines enjoy trying to get across: ultimately, the more you know, the more you realize just how little you know. And what a pleasure it is to caress time and again—with eyes, nose, or taste buds—this eternally renewed mystery.

Winemaking requires a whole gamut of skilled specialists ranging from the vineyard manager who organizes work on the soil and vines, to the cellarmaster who supervises the various stages of production from harvesting to bottling (with the guidance of oenologists), to brokers and traders who buy and market the finished wine, and finally either to retail merchants who target a specific clientele or to wine stewards who strive to serve diners in the best conditions. All of these professions are increasingly performed by women, such as this cellarmaster at Château Lagrezette in Cahors (*right*), who is drawing wine into a pipette in order to taste it. *Following pages*: The traditional method of pouring sherry into glasses in a cellar in Jerez, Spain (*left*), and the Schloss Johannisberg vineyard in Germany's Rhine region (*right*), which straddles the 50th parallel, the northernmost limit for planting wine-grapevines.

The Long Wine Route

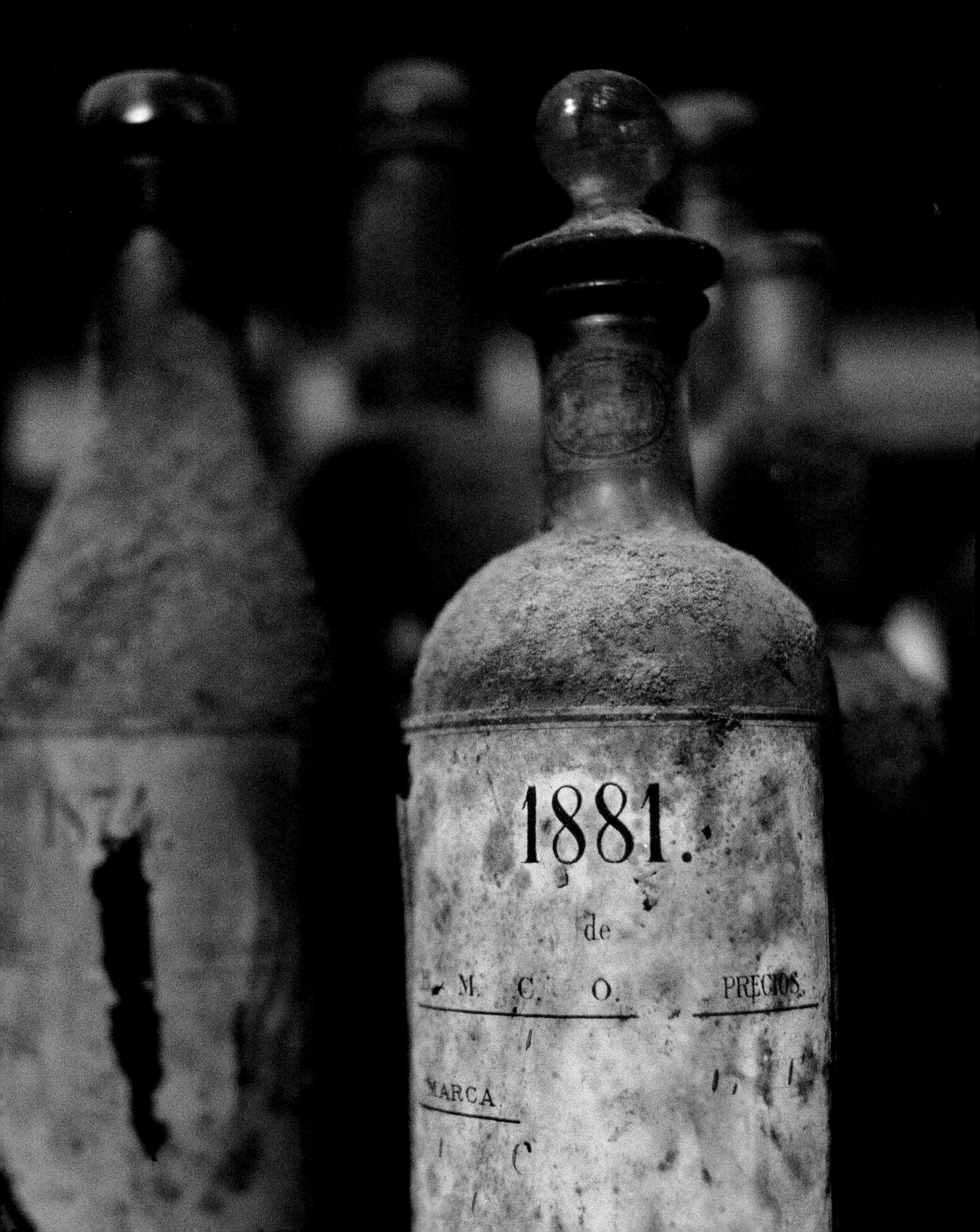
1881.
de
M. C. O.
PRECIOS.
MARCA.

The quest undertaken by all historians and scholars interested in wine and grapes has taken them to the sources of the Tigris and the Euphrates, to the hillsides and narrow silty plains of Armenia, and over into the Caucasian foothills of Georgia. Every archaeological find, every botanical study, every historical trace has led eventually to these cradles of Indo-European society, which is hardly surprising since wine seems intimately linked to the history of these civilizations, playing a constant role in their slow and chaotic development. It was the custom of the Caucasians of ancient times—that is of some half a dozen millennia ago—to sheath vine shoots in silver or precious metals before placing them in graves to accompany the dead on their last voyage. Wine has often defied time: archaeologists have found many amphoras in Egyptian, Greek, and Roman tombs, designed to refresh both the deceased and any gods encountered in the next world. While nowadays we might have our doubts about the usefulness of wine in the next life, we are still mighty proud to open a fine bottle which has been handed down over several generations.

Although heavenly virtues are sometimes attributed to it, wine interests historians precisely because it always echoes the rumblings of the earthly kingdom. Caucasian peasants who grew grapes sold, or at least bartered, the product of their harvest. A means of exchange, a commodity less perishable than most other foodstuffs, a drink endowed with fortifying properties, wine was one of the first consumer goods, along with livestock and grains, to fuel commerce between peoples and stimulate human exchange, either as trade in peacetime or as booty in war.

The commerce in wine at any given period and in any country provides special testimony to local habits, passions, and concerns, from Armenia ten thousand years ago through ancient Egypt and Etruria, to monasteries in Burgundy and in the Rhine and Mosel Valleys during the Middle Ages, to Renaissance Tuscany, across the eighteenth century not only in Bordeaux's vineyards but also in the busy, monied City of London, up to today's modern valleys in Chile, South Africa, and California.

"Wine, that most pleasant of beverages—which we owe either to Noah, who planted the vines, or to Bacchus, who pressed the grape juice—dates back to the world's infancy," explained gourmet writer Anthelme Brillat-Savarin in the early nineteenth century. Wine played a key role in many ancient cultures and especially in those religions on which our civilizations are based: from the sacred liquor of the Hindu god Brahma, *vêna* (from which the word for wine is derived in almost every European language to—of course—the Greek god Dionysus and his Roman counterpart Bacchus, gods of vegetation and eternal rebirth, and gods of life, symbolized by drunkenness and the cult of wine. *Above*: Bacchus on a cameo-like plaque from the Augustan period in Rome (Musée du Petit Palais, Paris). *Left*: A venerable bottle of vintage Gonzalès Byass sherry.

THE ORIGINS OF WINE

If wine can pride itself on such historical and geographic universality, this is above all because it comes from a plant with surprising powers of adaptation. The first species of grapevine appeared some sixty million years ago. Historians and researchers have attempted to trace it back as best they can, but the plant takes a mischievous delight in clouding its origins through multiple hybrids and multifarious layers of complex genetic evolution. Botanists specializing in the field once known as "ampelography" (from the Greek, "description of vines") have catalogued types and established collections that now testify to over 5,000 varieties of wine-producing grapevines, known by over 24,000 names depending on region and period. It becomes clear that identifying the first ancestor of this prolific family is an exercise hardly less breathtaking than tracing the origins of humanity.

Today's grapes, which go by the names of Cabernet Sauvignon, Syrah Chardonnay, Chenin Blanc, Pinot Noir, Cinsault and many others more or less well known to wine lovers, all belong to the large family known as *Vitis vinifera* (the name given by Swedish naturalist Carolus Linnaeus, who developed botanical nomenclature in the eighteenth century). The family can trace its roots back to the southern Caucasus in central Asia, between the Caspian Sea and the Persian Gulf. This ancestor then divided into three types.

The first became established in central Asia and the Near East—its fine bunches of table grapes became the Chasselas and seedless Sultana varieties that we now consume with delight. The second took root in Mesopotamia, Asia Minor and Armenia, to be spread by the Sumerians and Assyrians to the Georgian shores of the Black Sea, then by the Phoenicians as far as Europe; with its compact bunches of middling-sized grapes, this variety

developed into Cinsault, Clairette from southern France, and the small Corinth grapes which, like Sultanas, are seedless. The third type, dubbed *Vitis occidentalis*, accompanied the rise of the western civilizations that cultivated it. Born in the upper valley of the Nile, it grew up in the Mediterranean basin and ultimately settled throughout western Europe, from the Atlantic coasts of Portugal and France to the valleys of Germany. This is the ancestor of today's Pinots and Cabernets.

Evidence of the existence of these ancestral grapes has been found in fossils of seeds and pollen dating from the dawn of the Tertiary period. Because of their tendrils, these tough, wild vines clung to trees in the forests and grew toward the sun's rays, easily reaching a height of some 100 feet. Anyone interested in picking up their trail can find distant cousins still growing along the rivers of the Basque country. No one today would ever think of producing wine from such species; people, however, must have eaten the grapes, since piles of seeds have been found in caves that served as shelters in paleolithic times.

In the Quaternary period, glaciers slid over the surface of the globe for a million years, covering northern Europe before they withdrew once more. Grapevines, which detest both harsh cold and drought, took refuge in southern Europe, central Asia, and northern Africa. As the glaciers successively advanced and retreated, so the plant's terrain shrank and expanded. The glaciers no sooner withdrew than the vines returned to the newly warmed regions, thereby encountering other species and giving birth to new varieties. In the next-to-last ice age—the most intense—the cold drove the plant out of Europe completely. It sought shelter in central Asia, between the Caucasus and the Himalayas. During the final, somewhat gentler, period of glaciation, the grapevine adopted the Mediterranean region as its home.

This illustration shows the Malbec variety of grape. In the past two centuries, scientific study of the various types of grapes has attempted to organize them into families, tracing their origins and historical implantation in an effort to identify close relatives and distant cousins, the better to produce hybridization between species and perform genetic cloning. But the primary task of this science is to describe every variety as accurately as possible: not only how each one differs from others in terms of the color and shape of the grapes, the appearance and thickness of the skin, the shape of the bunch, and the size and form of the leaves, but also its resistance to disease, its productivity, the time of the year it ripens, its levels of sugar, tannins, acidity, and so on.

Thanks to its adaptability and readiness to reproduce through cuttings—it was enough simply to take a vine shoot and plant it where it was likely to grow—grapevines followed the wanderings of the nomads, the crusades of the Middle Ages, sixteenth-century merchants who transported Malvasia grapes throughout the Mediterranean basin, and later the missionaries and conquistadors who took the plant to Latin America, and the Dutch who shipped it to South Africa on their way to India in the seventeenth century.

It is not hard to picture the circumstances of mankind's initial encounter with wine. A few bunches of half-crushed grapes sitting in their own juices and forgotten for a few days would soon have fermented into a syrupy liquor which our ancestors must have found easily as palatable as the natural product of fermented dates or crushed wheat mixed with water. Over the centuries, the intense activity surrounding the harvesting of grapes was depicted in sculptures, tablets, sarcophagi, friezes, tapestries and paintings. A fine example may be seen in the bas-reliefs on the columns of the ancient theater in Arles, France, executed before 50 CE, showing baskets overflowing with grapes. But historian Marcel Lachiver looks much further back in time, attributing the first incontrovertible trace of winemaking to a press found near Damascus, Syria, believed to date back to the sixth millennium BCE.

Other historians place their bets on Armenia, where they claim the oldest vines have been found. They also cite the powerful symbolism of Noah planting a vine shoot after the Flood, at the very spot where he disembarked from his ark at Ararat, in Armenia, and getting drunk on the wine he made. Whatever the case, written cuneiform evidence indisputably confirms the existence of grapevines and wine in Mesopotamia in the fourth millennium BCE. As early as this, beer was rivalling as the most popular drink. In Babylonia—located in southern Mesopotamia, or present-day Iraq—grains formed the staple food, and bread and coarsely ground cereals soaked in water for a while produced a refreshing drink with euphoric effects that became highly popular among the natives. Very soon, wine nevertheless became an object of trade and transportation. In 2350 BCE, the king of the city of Lagash in Mesopotamia wanted his cellar to be filled

This Gallo-Roman bas-relief shows a merchant displaying casks and goatskins of wine to his clientele (Musée Archéologique, Dijon). Wine was brought to Gaul (modern-day France) by the Romans, and was immediately a great success both in terms of consumption and of production. Roman wines were white, or rather golden, usually very sweet because the grapes were picked late, and the best of them were drunk after several years of aging. The Gauls notably pioneered the use of wooden casks, initially employed by certain tribes to pour hot pitch on top of besieging forces from high fortifications, but later, from the beginning of the Christian era, put to more peaceful uses as containers for wine.

with large jars of wine brought from the upper country, that is to say the territory extending from the Mediterranean to the foothills of the Caucasus. He had his wish inscribed in stone, so providing evidence of a royal thirst that has survived to this day. The wine was shipped by caravans or boats up and down the Tigris and Euphrates, just as it would be for dozens of centuries afterwards. People in these lands —who have left behind some of the oldest cooking recipes—would already speak of the strength or delicacy of a wine, even distinguishing young wines from old, ordinary wines from those with "good taste," sweet wines blended with honey from those that were bitter, pale wines from those that had the color of a "bull's eye," and one regional wine from another (Tupliash, Arabânu, Karkemish, Simir, or Hilbunu). In the kingdom of Mari, not far from Babylon, the king kept considerable reserves of wine locked and guarded, distributing this nectar as a special drink to honor allies, soldiers, servants, and diplomatic envoys.

Egypt in turn began producing wine during the fourth dynasty, around 2,500 BCE, from grapes planted in the fertile soil of the Nile Valley. The Greeks also had a very ancient tradition of cultivating vines, as carbonized seeds dating from the fifth millennium have been discovered. In northern Greece, around Samos, Mytilene and Troy, Muscat grapes were certainly used to make wines that Homer described as "sweet as honey."

Amphorae recovered from the ocean floor have added further pieces to this jigsaw, put back together over the centuries. Around Marseille, containers dating from the last centuries BCE, still impregnated with marc, or wine residue, bear witness to the trade that linked Greece and Gaul, a commerce that extended into the interior of the continent, where incredible quantities of broken amphorae have come to light. With the arrival of the Romans just prior to the Christian era, vine-growing and winemaking would invade Gaul and then all the barbarian lands, thereby confirming wine's consistent if curious role as faithful companion to the rise of civilization.

There would be little point in trying to detail here all the stages in the history of wine, for an entire book would not suffice: first the steady establishment of vineyards throughout western Europe, from the Roman conquest to the Middle Ages, under the aegis of religious orders and feudal lords; then improved conditions and means of transportation which, from the Renaissance onwards, made it easier to recognize quality vintages and signalled the decline of vineyards too far to the north; next, the numerous grapevines loaded onto the galleons of the conquistadors, who introduced grape cultivation to Latin America; the subsequent revolution in trade and free-market policies in seventeenth- and eighteenth-century England, which was directly responsable for the remarkable of wines of great vintages; the golden age of both mass-produced and highly select wines during the Industrial Revolution, immediately followed by the total destruction of European vineyards by the aphid known as phylloxera; the startling development of quality vineyards in New World countries, from America to Oceania, during the second half of the twentieth century; and finally the new golden age of great wines from every continent as the second millennium draws to a close.

Above: Exekias, *The Sea Voyage of Dionysus*, painted ceramic cup (Antikensammlungen, Munich). Under the auspices of Dionysus, the Greeks developed the first true wine culture. Ritual festivals were an important part of life during winter and early spring, beginning with the Country Dionysia held in December, when each village celebrated the grape harvest with a procession led by a giant phallus, followed by the Great (or City) Dionysia in March, the occasion of delirious orgies. Every region of Greece had its vineyards, but some were already more celebrated than others, such as Methymne on the island of Lesbos. The Greeks always diluted their wine with water, and flavored it with various plants, flower essences, and even pine resin (a tradition that survives today in the form of the famous retsina). *Following pages*: Bimbi Bartolomeo (1648–1730), *Thirty-Eight Varieties* (Palazzo Pitti, Florence). Some of these varieties, such as Malvasia and Trebbiano, are still widely planted in Tuscany.

1 Lugliola.
2. Paſſerina roſſa.
3. Paſſerina bianca.
4. Moſcadella roſſa
5 Moſcadell bianc
6 Galletta bianca
7 Galletta nera
8 Moſcado di Candia
bianco

10. Di tre
11 Pietro
12 Malva
13 Regin
14 Spagn
15 Claret
16 Clare
17 Grec

These few images, events and trends are all milestones that have marked, at least temporarily, the long route taken by wine. Some of them will later serve to illustrate the various themes discussed in this book. The history of wine remains intimately linked to that of mankind, since the latter created the former and became intoxicated by it. Wine often provides insights into the economic ventures of western civilization, for, from antiquity to the present day, it has been one of those consumer goods whose trade has been most varied, most active and most naturally geared to export. It also sheds interesting light on the history of religion, from the powerful biblical symbolism of wine to the temporal power generated by the church's vast vineyards during the Ancien Régime. Wine has also been a companion to artists and poets from Bacchus to Omar Khayyam and from Rabelais to Baudelaire, whether with elegance or in excess. More dependably than the dates of wars or treaties, wine offers one of the most valuable keys to understanding how the people of any wine-consuming or -producing country or period lived. And just occasionally, this simple alcoholic beverage is more than just a key, by actually embodying history itself, through its ability to outlive the civilizations that created wine.

Depending on period and civilization, wine has appeared on dining tables in many and various guises, from the frankly excessive to the exquisitely refined (*right*). The seventeenth century in France certainly marked the start of the true beginnings of wine connoisseurship, in terms of the manner of serving as well as the quality of wine itself, as illustrated in Jacques Autrau's painting of the poet Alexis Piron dining with his friends Jean Vadé and Charles Collé, titled the *Wine Drinkers* (*above*). Piron did not hesitate to praise the simple pleasures of wining and dining in lively verses: "We wish long life to our local abbot / Who's abandoned the cross for the dining habit. / It's his service, my faith, that truly amazes/ And saves our refectory from the blazes. / The old abbot's Latin was very fine / But the new one—good soul—is conversant in wine!"

GREAT WINES NEVER DIE

The eastern flank of Hungary, not far from its current borders with Slovakia (to the north), Ukraine (to the east), and Romania (to the south), has been home to the Tokay vineyards for centuries, probably since Celtic times. This small region in the heart of a forgotten Europe contains somewhat fewer than 12,000 acres of vineyards, yet nevertheless produced one of the most vaunted, and perhaps most famous, vintages in the world. At imperial courts and princely banquets, people adored this silky, golden nectar with and aromatic smoothness that seduced the most refined of palates. Reserved for the elite of one of the world's two superpowers for nearly half a century, Tokay —or Tokaji in Hungarian—is now returning to favor among connoisseurs everywhere, with the added aura of mystery surrounding a rare wine last tasted by our ancestors, if they were lucky, in the early twentieth century. Such a comeback is a miracle in itself, since this pearl of central Europe has had to cope with wars, changing borders, imperial successions, Nazi exterminations, and periods of communist terror and/or bureaucracy, not to mention painful restructurings that have resulted from swiftly imposed but hard-to-digest freemarket policies. None of these vagaries, however, has ever managed permanently to extinguish the spark of genius that glitters in the heart of those golden bottles.

The region of Tokaji-Hegyalja (literally, "at the foot of the mountain"), attracted the attention of princes and kings early on,

and alternated periods of extreme prosperity with times of crisis. From the very earliest years of its fame, the startling likeness of the wine's brilliant color to the reflections of gold has never failed to impress. This, inevitably, made it an object of desire: the Tartars, who invaded and pillaged the country in 1241, emptied the wine cellars and devastated the vineyards. As the region had become depopulated, the Hungarians kings sent for Italian and Walloon colonists, renowned for their winemaking skills. Feudal lords and the clergy—the major landowners—along with the rich merchants of northern Hungary understood the vineyard's potential, even if they did not yet conceive of the wine as a luxury product.

It required yet another of those hard knocks to which the country has, alas, become accustomed—this time in the fifteenth century—for Tokay to take off in a dramatic and lasting fashion. While the Turks were busy invading the rest of Hungary, and most notably all the other wine-producing regions, the northeast was spared, to become, over time, a place of refuge for an alarmed, though not destitute, population. Noble families saw the area as an attractive, comfortable place of retreat, with a mild climate and gentle landscape. So whereas the rest of the country underwent a painful partition between the Turks, the Habsburgs, and the principality of Transylvania, Tokaji-Hegyalja became a haven of peace and prosperity as the sixteenth century dawned.

Landowners such as the Austrian emperor, the bishop of Eger, the kings of Hungary, and wealthy Hungarians and Poles lost

Several types of wine are produced in the Tokaji region, from dry white wines (less well known than their sweeter counterparts, but possessing true finesse), to an intermediate off-dry wine, to a range of thick sweet wines, more or lessrich in sugar. True Tokay is produced using a given percentage of over-ripe grapes called *aszu*; the word *puttonyos* (meaning basket) on the label indicates the proportion of *aszu* grapes in the wine, ranging from one to six *puttonyos*, the last being the sweetest and most sought-after. *Right:*This very long pipette, with a bulb at the hilt, is used by cellarmasters to sample wine often aged in a half-filled cask, beneath a natural "veil" not dissimilar to the one that forms on sherry.

no time in transforming their holdings into vast, ambitious vineyards. Polish merchants meanwhile offered them easy and rewarding markets for their wine. The princely Rakoczi family (which owned two-thirds of the vineyards) firmly established the tradition of Tokay and offered it the gift of virtually indefinite aging by hollowing cellars out of the chalky hills. It was at this point also, around 1570, that the discovery of *aszu* grapes was made (that is to say, grapes left to wither and die on the vine, like Corinth raisins, before being attacked by the helpful fungus known as "noble rot," used in Sauternes) and the luscious wine began its ascent to greatness. In the vineyards, this rise translated into the birth of a strict, organized hierarchy, in which the vineyards were guarded like strongboxes. High society circles snapped up the small, precious bottles, which were to be found crowning the tables of kings in all the courts of Europe and Russia. Louis XIV dubbed the wine with its definitive sobriquet—*vinum regum, rex vinorum* ("wine of kings, king of wines"). The Tokay trade even financed Ferenc Rakoczi's war against the Habsburgs; but when he emerged defeated in 1711, he was forced to forfeit his lands and go into exile. The wind now shifted. The new landowners, loyal to the court of Austria, were usually absent. They brought in German colonists to repopulate the area, and showed little interest in the wine, which they placed in the hands of traders who were also often foreigners, the original Poles being joined by Russians (who opened an outpost in Tokay to supply the czars

with quality wine), Greeks, and Armenians. Then came Jewish merchants who, thanks to their commercial dynamism, brought new prosperity to the wine and the region. The crown even took protectionist measures to combat forgeries, regulate the appellation area, and prevent foreigners from buying *aszu* grapes and vines.

In the first half of the nineteenth century, the marketing of Tokay suffered from the stormy relations between European nations—any producer tempted to export had to contend with heavy taxes, the fickleness of importing countries, the innumerable and exasperating customs points seperating Hungary's hereditary provinces, and the intrigues of the chamber of commerce in Vienna. At a time when vineyards in western Europe were experiencing heady growth, Hungarian vintners and traders could only bemoan these bureaucratic impediments. In 1867, the local traders' official almanac, the *Tokay Album*, contained the following observation: "We are blamed with being backward in marketing wine and cultivating vineyards. We are expected to rival eagles, but they clip our wings!"

Even when human destructiveness declared a truce, nature was capable of taking over in diabolical fashion: in the late nineteenth century, Tokay was ravaged by the phylloxera that laid waste all the vineyards of Europe. The vines had to be replanted, starting from scratch. Then the First World War devastated the region; the 1920 Versailles Treaty amputated Hungary of two-thirds of its territory, marking the end of an empire and the-

The European vogue for Tokay was enormous from the seventeenth century onwards, especially in Russia and France. In the eighteenth century, Tokay was considered the finest wine in the world. A royal gift par excellence, it was famous throughout all the courts of Europe, as illustrated by a letter from Voltaire to Madame de Pompadour in 1747: "Might not this tokay with which your excellency regaled me in Etioles bear some resemblance to the king who offered it? Like him, it is unadulterated, like him it combines strength with gentleness. Like him it delights the eye, enchants the heart, does good, and never changes." *Left*: French oenologist Alain Rousse in the wine cellar of Château Megyer.

reby limiting the ambitions of its finest produce. Nazi infamy put a permanent end to the activities and very existence of the community of Polish Jewish merchants who had bolstered the region's fame and prosperity for centuries. These wounds had not yet healed when the Bolshevik millstone destroyed the last remaining vestiges of the great tradition of Tokay as a work of art. Although trade boomed—the Soviet "big brother" was a prolific consumer of wines and spirits—considerations of quality were totally ignored. In order to encourage large, highly productive vineyards, the hilly slopes were abandoned for the less well-exposed but easier-to-work plains, where the heavy soils were less suited to high quality vines. To facilitate production and avoid the risks (but also the benefits) of maturation, the wine was pasteurized, which amounted to eliminating everything that contributed to its character and personality. To come into line with collectivist doctrine and to simplifying the packaging and shipment of the wine to a single client, producers and vineyards were all grouped together to form one winery designed to yield a single wine. Hungarian resembles no other language, but the word used to describe this cooperative hegemony is redolent of both the period and its Soviet origins: *kombinat*, or industrial combine.

And yet, the Tokay region and its humble residents held out with intense, unsuspected strength. In 1989, when communism collapsed, the cards were dealt anew—the first foreign investors moved in, the winemakers recovered ownership of their parcels of vines, and improvised in their garages. French insurance companies and investors from Spain, Britain, and later America and Hong Kong discovered the magic of the golden wine, even though the return on their investment was to be far from immediate: the vines had to be replanted, yields had to be cut back to reasonable levels, and wineries had be rebuilt with modern equipment. The wine for its part does not fulfill its potential every year (the precious *aszu* grapes are not easy to obtain), and even when it is thick and smooth it requires a minimum of three years of aging in the cask. Nevertheless, it has recovered its ancestral ability to overcome every setback and tragedy, even attracting some of Bordeaux's leading producers of equally sweet Sauternes. Such investors, however, represent only 10% of the total vineyard, and the *kombinat*—now dubbed State Farm—still counts 10,000 small producers.

In this land of oblivion, where individual and collective memories have been obliterated, everyone now strives to re-create the original Tokay, all the while hoping to adapt it to modern tastes in order to boost sales and recover the prosperity of previous centuries. Thus can wine sometimes transcend the memory of individuals, endowing the genes of those who serve it with the pride and talent of their forebears. Time, in this case, must be measured on a scale which has nothing to do with immediate history.

Above: The new cellar at Disnökö, one of the largest Tokay vineyards, bought and rebuilt in 1990 by the AXA insurance company (which also owns several estates in Bordeaux). The modernity and cleanliness of this cellar is startling in a region where private wine-producing cellars are still very rare and generally under-equipped. It nevertheless perfectly complements an installation boasting extensive underground cellars, similar to the one in the museum at Tolcsva (*right*), where thousands of bottles from every vintage slumber on shelves swathed in ancestral moss, black and damp. These endless tunnels carved from the region's limestone bedrock centuries ago provide high humidity and constant temperature, insuring that the wine will age perfectly.

Above:The Thelema Mountain vineyard at Stellenbosch. Vineyards have a long history in South Africa, since the Dutch colonists who founded Cape Town on the southwestern tip of the country imported the first plants in 1659. Soon afterward, a small town some twelve miles south of the Cape, named Constantia after the wife of a governor of the province in the late seventeenth century, began producing a sweet white wine that would enjoy a dazzling success in Europe in general and England in particular, starting in the eighteenth century and peaking in the latter half of the nineteenth. The boom in South African wine production was also boosted by the arrival of many French Protestants from wine-growing regions, who were driven by persecution into Holland, and then onto the new colonies.

Stellenbosch, to the east of Cape Town, was the center of French Protestant winemaking, along with Paarl and Franschoek. The region offers great potential for the production of good wine: its fields are well exposed and easy to work, its temperate climate is hot and dry during the austral summer, and the harvest is rarely disturbed by heavy rain, thanks to steady weather conditions year after year. These vineyards now produce a number of white wines, often made from the Chenin Blanc grape originally from the Anjou and Touraine regions of France, as well as German and Alsatian varieties such as Traminer and Riesling. Fresh, fruity, balanced and aromatic, these wines still for the most part lack a highly developed personality, but their return to the world stage with the end of apartheid should inspire new ambitions.

THE QUEST FOR QUALITY

Whatever the advantages they may owe to their birthright, the history's truly great figures of history have always forged their own destinies. The same holds good for vineyards and wines. True enough, the wine-growing regions of Europe have benefited from a tremendous head-start in establishing their reputations and the benefits accorded by soil and sky by nature vary from place to place and time to time; and yet no wine has ever become famous overnight. Success has to be built up gradually, reflecting not only the dynamism and commitment of the people who give the vineyards life, but also, and above all, the evolution and intensity of the wine-loving public's taste.

When wine went global in the second half of the twentieth century, a new attitude emerged, which involved the regulation of wine and the application of industrial levels of consistency. Since the Industrial Revolution of the nineteenth-century, agriculture everywhere had of course flirted with similar techniques, and European winemakers were not among the last to consider turning their craft into a mass industry. But they always remained just one part of the overall business: the jug of red or the quick glass at the bar (inexpensive brands employing advertising as gaudy as it was efficient) could co-exist—without making contact, either in reality or in the minds of consumers—with châteaus, cellarmasters, and local vintages. The two worlds existed side by side without ever meeting—one marching at the hectic pace of wine freighters unloading floods of Algerian wine in the port of Rouen and of feverish Parisian dealers at the Bercy depot, while the other following the rhythm of the seasons and the respiration of the soil.

Those who pioneered wine's new frontiers in America, Oceania and Africa could not have cared less about such distinctions. They went industrial because all agricultural business in those free-trade, productivity-driven markets worked that way. Given land where the smallest farm can boast corn fields stretching for dozens of miles, or where a modest hacienda has livestock numbering in the thousands, it is hard to imagine how people in California, Argentina, or Australia could have thought in terms other than big, pragmatic, mechanized. One of the main differences between these two approaches relates to the very philosophy of production: craft wine-growers exploit—or are subject to—the specific features of local soil and the whims of climate, as they slowly construct a style for their wine; in contrast, industrial wine-growers seek to limit the effect of all parameters external to the ones they themselves have introduced. Wine-growers in the Châteauneuf-du-Pape district near Avignon, for example, have adapted over the centuries to the warm soil and very dry climate by planting varieties of grapes able to withstand this kind of climate and the accompanying scarcity of water, from which they have managed to produce red wines that are generous, powerful, and highly distinctive. Given similar climatic conditions, industrial producers would seek instead to counter the sole negative factor in that equation, namely drought. Installing a drip irrigation system in the vineyard would obviously add significantly to production costs,

Left: The Australian vineyards of Marananga, in Barossa Valley, a few dozen miles north of Adelaide in the state of South Australia, combines rows of vines with palm trees. The climate is sunny and hot, although not nearly so extreme as in the central and northern regions of this island-continent, where drought makes any agricultural activity impossible. The relatively cool temperatures of the coastal zone, as in Coonawarra further south, has encouraged the planting of vineyards, which have enjoyed a spectacular boom in recent decades. Now, Australia appears along with Chile, to be one of the most promising wine-growing countries. *Above*: Lionel Lecomte, a wine steward from Burgundy, using sight and touch to assess the quality of the year's harvest.

but it would also confer the sovereign right to plant whatever variety they desired, notably the one which best reflects market trends at any given moment.

This latter approach would be perfect if great wines did not possess, in addition to all the qualities of their composition and flavor, one supreme attraction than can never be offered by the most productive of industries —the genius of being unlike any other product. Some New World producers realized this fact relatively quickly. With a certain pride, California has seen its large industrial outfits take a back seat—although hardly bowing out—to small vineyards where people know how to cultivate distinctive wines that combine to the full the strengths of the soil with the inventive talent of the winemaker. Other coun-

tries are joining this search for heightened quality with surprising swiftness. The very pragmatism of industrial growers sometimes spurs them to become pure craft winemakers.

In this respect, the history of Chilean vineyards is edifying and ultimately rather encouraging for the future. Ever since the first grapevines were introduced into the country by the Spanish conquistadors in 1550, Chilean winemaking has alternated between periods of glory and periods of crisis. A number of protectionist laws were passed in the often lively political climate of the twentieth century, and it was only in 1974 that the prohibition on new planting was finally lifted. Civil upheavals clearly had an impact on the daily life of winegrowers, as the Chilean dictatorship heralded an era of unbridled free-trade preached by its

Composed of a narrow strip of land less than 150 miles wide between the Pacific Ocean and the Andes mountain range, yet stretching several thousand miles from north to south, Chile is an almost self-sufficient country with fertile soil and a sheltered climate. Vines earned a privileged place early on, although the country's wines have only attained leading status in terms of quality and ambition in recent years. The vineyards are concentrated in valleys sloping down to the sea, notably in Aconcagua province to the north of Santiago (the capital), in Santiago province itself (especially along the Maipo Valley), and finally further south along the valleys of the Itata and Bio-Bio. *Left*: The Vina Aquitania winery, founded by two French wine-growers from Médoc, Paul Pontallier (director of Château Margaux) and Bruno Prats (owner of Château Cos d'Estournel). *Above*: The vineyards of Vina Santa-Emiliana.

squads of "Chicago boys." Vines were planted and wine flowed, everyone in Chile (as elsewhere) hoping to hit the jackpot in the rush to produce liquid gold. Naturally, a surfeit was produced. And this surplus soon coincided with a catastrophic fall in local consumption, leading to economic crisis.

In the late 1980s, having just managed to emerge from this debacle thanks to a policy of converting large numbers of mediocre vineyards to the cultivation of table grapes, the Chileans—no longer content with their domestic market—decided that they would set out to seduce consumers in other countries across the globe. Local wine-growing was restructured as in any other modern industry: traditional firms invested in new equipment, enabling them to improve the quality of their wines, and established their own vineyards instead of simply buying the grapes of other growers, as they had long been accustomed to do; former producers of fruit or table wine meanwhile also acquired sophisticated equipment; and many French and a few American investors became aware of Chile's incalculable potential and mounted joint-venture operations. Today, every single one of the sixty main *bodegas* (cellars) boasts a battery of stainless steel vats and a full range of technology designed to develop high quality wines.

Chilean wines initially eased their way into a price/quality gap at the precise moment when the most dynamic producer-countries were experiencing difficulties. Spain and Australia were hit by drought, France was undergoing a chaotic period of years of frost or rain,

VINTAGE 1992   BOTTLED MAY 1996
Bottle   of a total of 30,216 Bottles
Magnum   of a total of 600 Magnums

Heitz Cellar

NAPA VALLEY
CABERNET SAUVIGNON
ALCOHOL 13.5% BY VOLUME
PRODUCED AND BOTTLED IN OUR CELLAR BY
HEITZ WINE CELLARS
ST. HELENA, CALIFORNIA, U.S.A.

and California was invaded by phylloxera. For only a few dollars a bottle, Chile's mainly red wines combined fruitiness with rich texture and forthrightness, making an immediate not only to Americans (who rapidly promoted Chile to third place on their favorite wine imports, after Italy and France), but also to the British, the Canadians, and northern Europeans. Chile's wine exports increased thirteen-fold between 1991 and 1997, and are now sold in some 100 countries.

Commercial success has been accompanied by heightened ambitions. Now that they are key players in the wine business, Chilean producers want to join a new club, the much more select one of great vintage wines. Ten years after its first transformation, Chile is undergoing another one: wine-growers are seeking out favorable sites and smaller yields, great red varieties are being blended rather than bottled separately, and the skills and knowledge of master winemakers and oenologists are being brought in from Bordeaux, the Loire, Burgundy, and California.

The first Chilean wine retailing for $50 per bottle in the United States (as against the normal average of $5 to $7), was launched early in 1998 by one of the old local firms, Errazuriz, in partnership with the Californian winemaker Robert Mondavi. Many other *bodegas* have been preparing offensives in recent years, some of them already bringing to market wines twice the price and quality of those sold at the start of the decade. Now they lack only that element that can be neither bought nor found—experience.

New World vineyards have barely had time to establish the reputations of their finest producing regions, so wine-growers, estate owners and merchants have been all the more assiduous in making their names or brands known. Some, such as Heitz from California (*above*), have acquired a reputation comparable to the most famous European wine producers, based on limited production from grapes picked in their own vineyard (rather than bought from elsewhere in the area) and on a location in the best part of the region, Napa Valley. Other producers, like Chilean Errazuriz (*right*, vineyards and cellar) staking their bets on agreements with other firms—in this case, the American Mondavi—to develop their international appeal.

NEW FRONTIERS

Wine-grapevines grow within rather strict geographical limits, namely the ones that define temperate climates. A globe indicating all the main areas of vineyards on the planet would reveal in striking fashion the invisible borders marking the vineyard zone: between 30° and 50° latitude in the northern hemisphere (the level of Vancouver and Reims to the north, or Los Angeles and Marrakesh to the south), and between 30° and 40° in the southern hemisphere (incorporating Chile and Argentina, the southern tip of South Africa, southern Australia and northern New Zealand). These climatic borders are nevertheless vast, insofar as they include almost all the most developed countries in the world, excluding Great Britain and Scandinavia.

In this context, one of the most startling aspects of the two last decades is the breathtaking growth of both vine-growing and wine appreciation. Countries that long resisted all western consumer products—apart from the two inevitable symbols of American capitalism, Coca-Cola and McDonald's—suddenly began, all at the same time, to buy vintage wines, either drinking wine at meals or regularly enjoying an aperitif of white wine or champagne. Newly rich sectors of society in countries that formerly made up the Eastern bloc now collect cases of the finest Bordeaux wines; the Japanese are slowly abandoning cognac and whisky in favor of fine red wines; Singapore, Taiwan and Hong Kong have become hubs of the wine trade. Even more surprising, China—still called the "People's

The angle of a vineyard's exposure to the sun is a critical factor in the quality of a wine, as it determines the ease with which grapes ripen. When New World farmers decided to plant wine-grapevines, they did exactly as their predecessors had done centuries earlier in every region of Europe, avoiding deep, narrow valleys and north-facing slopes, where sunshine is lacking early and late in the day. These Australian vineyards (*above*) in the broad, well-exposed Yarra Valley, planted on a site with the evocative name of Coldstream Hills, enjoy the cooling effect of running water to freshen grapes flooded with sunlight all day long.

Republic"—is spurring growth in both local vineyards and domestic consumption.

China is clearly waking up. Or at least, part of China—its big cities. You need only to fly into Shanghai to be convinced. As far as the eye can see, construction is going on at a frantic pace everywhere in this megalopolis of sixteen million inhabitants. Every hundred yards sees the demolition of a "shanty neighborhood" (whereas other countries have shanty "towns," Chinese cities tolerate the coexistence of luxury buildings and slum neighborhoods, side by side), as its residents are summarily evicted to other, outlying neighborhoods, and a construction site is inaugurated. Operating night and day, this will soon give birth to an impressive luxury building. Those nostalgic for the Shanghai of the 1930s, like those nostalgic for hard-line communism (if any remain), now search in vain here for kindred spirits: this country—or this part of it, at least—now obeys just one master, the great god Business.

Between the clever ones who realized what was happening before everyone else, those who are now waking up, and those who probably soon will, it is not difficult to see how China's big cities are currently producing a wealthy —very wealthy—class as well as a middle class destined to grow year by year. Obviously, all these people consume. And they consume a good deal. Boutiques featuring famous brands or designer clothes, beside department stores such as Galeries Lafayette, are not aimed at tourists alone—the stalls and pioneering supermarkets are thronged by local shoppers who snap up the cheaper items, usually pro-

Although sunshine is essential, the cool, stable temperatures associated with a nearby body of water are also highly prized assets for any vineyard. Rippon Vineyard, overlooking Lake Wanaka in New Zealand (*above*), benefits from mild temperatures even during cold spells, as does every vineyard near a river, lake or sea. Water remains warmer than the air in spring and fall, thus minimizing the risk of frost; thanks to the inverse phenomenon during summer, water cools the vineyard and enables the grapes to retain sufficient acidity. Finally, newer wine producers also take ease of production into account, sometimes abandoning sunny slopes in favor of vast alluvial plains, such as Montana's Brancolt estate in Blenheim, New Zealand (*following pages*).

duced locally. Although wine still plays a modest role, far behind the cheaper beer and wretched Chinese "wine" made from fermented sorghum, it is on the upswing. The Chinese, ever ready to adopt with alacrity products previously considered exotic, place enormous importance on the reputed medicinal values of what they eat. Here, as in the rest of Asia and much of the American continent, a medical study entitled "The French Paradox" lent sudden and powerful credentials of medical virtue to wine by demonstrating that the tannins in red wine can help prevent cardiovascular disease. Brands such as "Dynasty," "Great Wall," "Dragon Seal," "William Pitters" and "Asia"—all invented and established by big foreign firms (usually French)—are enjoying solid growth. These wines, with their "all-purpose" taste, are opening up new horizons. Produced in local vineyards, they are made by international technicians who exercise a pragmatic approach in adapting western principles to the local climatic conditions, and above all to the traditional practices of resident wine-growers.

SOLDIERS AND SORCERERS

World-wide conquest requires its soldiers. In new wine-producing countries from the United States to South Africa, a single individual, called the winemaker, combines the traditional tasks of a cellarmaster (who makes the wine on a day-by-day basis) and oenologist (a special consultant who conducts chemical and hygienic analyses). In countries where speed has been elevated to a fundamental value underlying the economy, the profession of winemaker has evolved swiftly: "flying winemakers" now zip from a vineyard in the northern hemisphere to a grape-harvest in the southern hemisphere, either on behalf of the estate itself or on behalf of a foreign buyer who has asked that a specific wine be produced. A good many flying winemakers from Australia and New Zealand are thus dispatched to the four corners of the world by British retail chains in order to produce wine perfectly suited to local consumers.

In the southern hemisphere, oenologists arrive before the grapes are picked (in January) and leave toward the end of May (depending on the year), which enables them to attend the birth of another wine, north of the equator, in September. Other regions, located closer to the tropics, afford even the possibility of producing a third wine; in Texas in particular, the grape-picking ceremony takes place between July and August.

To the eyes of a casual observer, the lives of flying specialists at the dawn of the third millennium have nothing in common with those

From as early as the eighteenth century wine proved itself capable of seducing the peoples of the Orient, if Usbek, the central character of Montesquieu's *Persian Letters* is to be believed. Writing to Rehdi, he declares (Letter XXXIII), "But if I disapprove of the use of this drink which makes us lose our reason, I do not similarly condemn those by which it is enlivened. The wisdom of the orientals lies in the fact that they seek as diligently for remedies against unhappiness as for those against the most dangerous diseases. When a European suffers some misfortune, he has no resource but to read a philosopher called Seneca; but Asians, showing more sense and a better knowledge of medicine, take drinks which can make a man cheerful and dispel the memory of his sorrows" (trans. C.J. Betts, Penguin: 1973). *Above*: Label of a Chardonnay produced by the Vergelegen winery in South Africa.

of winemakers who have respected time-honored practices for centuries, in order to make wine from their own vineyard. In place of the slow, immutable rhythm of life on the farm, flying winemakers embody the feverish pace of an epoch in which movement means life.

A modern winemaker might be commissioned by a British retailer

to go to South Africa to produce, with a team of six oenologists, a trifling 700,000 twelve-bottle cases of South African wine. Management in Britain will have signed contracts with a dozen cellars in the Cape area, obliging our winemaker to cover 15,000 miles in the space of six weeks in order to supervise all the operations. He or she rises at 6 a.m. in order to visit the first cellar—or rather, the vines themselves—in the company of a local, full-time specialist, where they survey specific plots, assess the grapes (for sugar and acid levels), and choose those corresponding to the wines they want to produce. The owners will probably haggle over relinquishing the finest bunches, especially if it looks as though the harvest will be modest. A deal may be done by swapping varieties—if the flying winemaker insists on getting those fine Cabernet grapes, for example, he will have to accept a double quantity of the much less prized Cinsault variety. Once the raw materials have been identified, another major operation involves repairing to the office to establish the winemaking procedures to be followed. It will then be up to the local cellarmaster to monitor the wine step by step, according to the instructions of the Australian or New Zealand specialist, who now has to dash off to other

cellars to offer advice. The specialist will return only later that day or the next, to make sure the local team is carrying out instructions correctly.

The challenge faced by flying winemakers assigned a specific mission in a specific region is to make sure that a harvest produces a decent wine whatever the circumstances. Whereas a traditional oenologist might be compared to a country doctor, modern specialists are more like physicians working for a humanitarian organization such as "Médecins Sans Frontières"—they must adapt to all situations and produce the desired result come what may.

And yet, despite being constantly on the move, they repeat the same dawn-to-dusk tasks performed by any sedentary oenologist during the harvest. They spend two to three hours in the fields in the morning, identifying the grapes to be picked the next day. They check the specific gravity of the vats, monitor the temperature of the must (as fermenting juice is called), taste it, and supervise reception of the day's harvest. They must apply the basic rules of winemaking occasionally under extreme conditions. Since they cannot know everything on arrival, they take a minimum of risks and a maximum of precautions, enabling them to produce a wine that is well made if without much character. And yet here again modern-day developments have swiftly elaborated a version of things closer to haute-couture fashion than to ready-to-wear clothes. These days, certain elite estates are calling in veritable designer winemakers, who do their utmost to bring out the very essence of the estate they are advising.

On every estate in the world, the fermenting room represents the crucial heart of wine production, for it is here that the grape juice ferments into alcohol. The fermenting room is usually vast—depending on production capacity—and filled with large vats specially reserved for fermentation (and, in the case of red wines, for maceration of the must with the skins of pressed grapes). The vat seen here (*right*) is part of the plant at Bodega San Pedro in Chile. Made of wood, the vat is open at the top to allow the carbon dioxide produced by fermentation to escape. *Above:* The reddened hands of a picker after a hard day's work at Saint Clement Vineyards in Napa Valley.

Frenchman Michel Rolland is undoubtedly the most famous of these new wine craftsmen, who flit with enthusiasm and delight, from one estate to another, from the creation of one nectar to another. Though he dresses with all the style of a Bordeaux estate owner, his stocky gait, ready smile and irrepressible *joie de vivre* are constant reminders that he has never stopped being a mischievous child of the surrounding countryside. Although a member of a guild of oenologists who are deliberately serious and austere in their comportment, Rolland relishes new experiments in unknown vineyards with the same appetite that he brings to a meal of roast duck with cepes mushrooms on his own Fronsac estate.

He is now consultant to some of Bordeaux's greatest vineyards—whose owners announce his arrival in the same proud tones adopted by the president of a soccer team revealing the name of his new coach—but also spends many weeks in California, Argentina, Chile, Italy, and even India. The task is always the same: Rolland observes the vineyard and assesses its qualitative potential, sets the date of harvest, advises on the winemaking procedure and monitors the major stages by constantly tasting the wines (relying more on his infallible tastebuds than on chemical analyses). Rolland goes far beyond the normal mission of a professional oenologist—supposed to help eliminate the risks and dangers that might threaten the development of a wine—because he understands better than most that a great wine is a unique product which must be given every possibility to express to the full its own soil and climate.

There are those who complain that Rolland and his acolytes have standardized the great red wines, all henceforth characterized by the expression of a ripe, fruity taste and tannins almost caramelized by oak casks, simply because: a) Rolland prefers to pick grapes when fully ripe rather than rush to harvest green fruit at the first drop of rain; b) he has brought back the old idea of aging great vintages in high quality casks rather than in old barrels of doubtful hygienic standards; and above all c) he has popularized these ideas among an increasing number of growers. Nothing could be more absurd than these unfounded accusations. Once the signs of youth have faded, these wines—developed from healthy, ripe grapes—express the profound uniqueness of their soil and climate better than any others. Paradoxically, it is great oenologists such as Rolland who have re-established, notably in the newer countries, the idea of the primacy of the soil and the fruit itself over pure wine-making techniques; there is no point in marshaling technical skills and sophisticated equipment if the raw material—in this case, the grapes—is of little worth. "When an owner asks me to advise him how to make a great wine, I always apply the same three rules," explains Rolland with his southern volubility. "First of all, I ask him to significantly reduce the yield of his vines. Then I suggest he display a little more patience before picking, until the bunches are perfectly ripe. Finally, when it comes to winemaking, my third principle is never to apply any principles. The winemaker must submit and adapt to his grapes." These

IIn *Mémoires d'un Touriste*, Stendhal describes the following scene: "A diner is being teased about his fortunate life—he is a wine broker. These gentlemen bring no capital to their trade other than a horse and tilbury. They scour the Médoc, a land that produces good wine, on the left bank of the Gironde River from Bordeaux to the Cordouan tower. They taste the owners' wine, and mark its quality on the cask with chalk. Just imagine how the owners court them. Woe to the owner who erases a broker's chalk mark! No broker will undertake to sell his wine." But brokers also played a more modest role—though just as useful—than the one described by Stendhal, as witnessed by this village broker in Cramant, Champagne in the 1950s (*left*). *Above*: Oenologist Michel Rolland, a modern judge of great wines.

rules are universal, because they are dictated by one that is even more universal: when it comes to wine, nothing great will emerge unless profound attention is paid to nature.

THE HEART OF THE MYSTERY

While to some people the world seems too small, to others an entire lifetime will not suffice to learn, with minute precision, the full potential of the few acres that compose their vineyard. Just as the discovery of the infinitely small can be as fascinating as that of the infinitely vast, so the mysteries of wine may remain as unfathomable at the level of a winemaker's cellar as they do on a continental scale.

The Rhône River is already wide as it flows between Vienne and Valence, but it retains the spirit of its Alpine origins, constantly taunting the granite of the Massif Central as it skirts the eastern flank of that ancient mountain range. Although the deep south is not far away, this valley is harsh, and the corridor separating north from south has never left much room for people living there to grow crops or set up businesses. In this difficult terrain, vines have ever since Roman times found their ideal growing conditions. On the steep slopes running down from the plateau of the Massif Central to the river, people have over the centuries levelled narrow terraces where one, two, or a maximum of three rows of grapevines might be planted.

Gérard Chave has devoted his life and talent to building—or rather consolidating, given its centuries-old existence—the reputation of the name Hermitage which, along with Côte Rôtie and Châteauneuf-du-Pape, produces some of the greatest vintages in the Rhône Valley. Like his father Jean-Louis (and like everyone else in the Chave family for centuries, and his own son), Gérard has a distinc-tive understanding of the hill called l'Hermitage, which overlooks the town of Tain-l'Hermitage. L'Hermitage is a granite peak rising on the edge of the Massif Central. In its wild youth, the Rhône decided to confront this natural obstacle head-on rather than flow around it, and managed to slice between the peak and the slope, so that the shaft of granite now stands alone on the left bank of the river, separated from the mountain that gave it birth, an impressive witness to the geological battles of primeval times.

Chave cultivates discretion. As you stumble across the dark façade of this village house with its faded sign over the door, you would hardly imagine that this modest family home conceals vast cellars containing some of the greatest treasures of France's vineyards. The interior of the house is equally modest, but the visitor's first view of the inner courtyard, reminiscent of traditional village schools (if the delightful bric-a-brac were removed), complete with covered playground and age-old plane tree, carries with it the scent of eternal, wonderful France. This sleepy spot needs a human spark to awaken it: the nimble, straightforward gaze of the master of the house, constantly enlivened by a hint of mischief, indulgence and good-heartedness immediately conveys a feeling of elation that seems to breathe life into his surroundings.

Gérard Chave likes nothing better than tasting his wines, as he accompanies his fortunate visitors, drawing wine from a cask with his pipette before decanting it into a glass. Each of the casks in the neatly ordered row contains the fruit of different plots on the hill. Every plot has its own name and every wine has its own formidable personality: Les Bessards has the vigor and power of the granite soil on which it grows. L'Ermite has the loftiness and finesse to be expected from the summit of the hill. Méal is rounder and smoother, while Rocoules and L'Homme hint at other

With its large, rounded pebbles like those found on beaches, few wine-growing areas possess a soil as striking as that found at Châteauneuf-du-Pape, at least in certain parts of this extensive region on the left bank of the Rhône River between Orange and Avignon. It was the river which once carried these pebbles across the alluvial plateaux, before retreating to its bed. The pebbles reflect the sun's rays toward the grapes and store the day's often torrid heat. Grapes thus ripen faster and attain high sugar levels, easily yielding an alcohol content of 13.5% to 14%. Fortunately, the cool northerly wind of the mistral offers relief to the vines, which might otherwise suffer from the relentlessly dry heat.

tales, and other flavors. Each vatful constitutes a superb wine on its own, and Chave is able to describe with great precision the location and exposure of any given row of vines. And yet, like his father and grandfather before him, Gérard Chave will blend—after long months in the cask—these highly expressive wines. From these various soils he will produce a single wine, quite simply eliminating the wines he thinks will disrupt the harmony of the ensemble (the remainder being sold in bulk to delighted merchants). Unlike the course manufacturers of Tokay in the days of communism, who blended all their output merely to avoid complicating life, Chave identifies and discloses every facet

of his vineyard in order to recompose it faithfully, later, in the bottle. This quest for perfection, shared by great winemakers throughout the world, is clearly the distinguishing factor which, in every clime, sets apart a great wine from the mass of good wines, and which separates the work of true craftsmen from run-of-the-mill manufactured products. It is no easy matter for a connoisseur to recognize these jewels immediately, for they require repeated tastings. Wine-growers, meanwhile, must follow a long apprenticeship to attain a perfect respect for their soil, their climate, their vines, and their wine. Which is precisely the subject of the chapters that follow.

For a winemaker, tasting is an essential way to monitor not only the work already accomplished but also, and above all, the development of the wine. Usually, tasting is done in the cellar by drawing a small quantity of wine from the cask with a pipette placed in the bunghole, as seen at Marcel Guigal's cellar in Ampuis (*left*), or through a special tap installed in steel or cement vats. A winemaker may also assess the way in which older wines are maturing, a process undertaken here by Charles Hours (*above*) with Jurançon wine from Clos Urolat. *Following pages*: Two famous vineyards—Pernand-Vergelesses, in the Côte de Beaune region of Burgundy (*left*) and the pebbly soil of Château Cos d'Estournel at Saint-Estèphe in Médoc.

Vine
and
Vineyard

When the first conquistadors landed on the unexplored continent of America, they tore their breeches on the dense undergrowth as they fought their way through the wild vines with woody stems stretching for dozens of yards along the ground, or using trees as supports to grow high into the air. Like the Hebrews who picked the miraculous fruit of Canaan, the Spaniards were soon harvesting bunches of grapes to make wine.

People have naturally encountered grapevines in every temperate zone and every period of history, either growing wild or cultivated under more or less sophisticated conditions. It is precisely because vines will grow almost anywhere that they have entered the collective unconscious of the western world so thoroughly. Anyone who has planted a young vine in the garden may well have been almost disconcerted by the ease with which the plant adapts and spreads. But everyone will also have observed that the quality of a wine is intimately linked to the spot where the vine grows.

THE MAGIC OF THE SOIL

Like all plants, vines basically feed on water, which their roots draw from the depths of the soil. Obesity in plants is unknown, since they do not like to overfeed—if the vines are sitting in water or if their roots penetrate directly into the water table, the apprentice grower who cultivates the vineyard will have no chance of producing any wine, as the roots will rot and the plant will die. Furthermore, the finest wine-growing soils are never the best terrain for most other plants domesticated as crops; while grains require rich and well-watered ground, and most fruit trees send out their roots horizontally, vines seem by contrast drawn down to the depths of the earth. The deeper the plant pushes its roots below the ground, the more firmly it anchors itself in the soil to find sustenance, the more it will tend to yield quality wines.

Of course, not all vineyards and not all growers are equally demanding. All over the world you may see vineyards growing on well wate-

Vines can grow happily in a great variety of soils and subsoils. The only point of similarity, for example, between the dry soil in the Côtes du Rhône region (*above*), covered with rounded pebbles washed across the landscape hundreds of thousands of years ago, and the heavier, clayey soils of Australia (*right*), is the fact that vines planted in both places produce excellent wines. Chalky, clayey, sandy, granitic, schisty, rocky, stony or pebbly—vines can adapt to all soils. But for each of these characteristics, the wine-grower will select the most suitable variety of grape, the most appropriate growing methods (notably those that allow the roots to penetrate most deeply), and decide whether or not to drain the land in order to facilitate water run-off and avoid erosion.

red plains, oceans of vines in impeccable rows, like a succession of waves never rocked by any storm. Yet these overly welcoming soils will never produce nectars of the quality of those that derive, for example, from the gritty, gravelly soil of Médoc.

Few regions illustrate better than Médoc the contribution of topsoil and subsoil to the creation of great wines. Home to the great Bordeaux wines of Margaux, Saint-Julien, Pauillac and Saint-Estèphe, Médoc is shaped like a long spit of land, running for some sixty miles along the left bank of the Gironde River, itself the broad and vast estuary of the Garonne River. This land is, of course, alluvial in origin, for centuries a marshy plain apparently unsuitable for any crops or even for human settlement.

In the Middle Ages, when Blaye and Bourg, on the opposite bank of the Gironde, were major towns with nearby vineyards producing reputable wines, Pauillac was just a humble fishing village, and no wine estates were to be found until you reached the outskirts of the city of Bordeaux. Over the millennia, the river had steadily carted and deposited subsoil and topsoil—centuries of clayish marl, of gravel brought down from their sources by streams and rivers, and of alluvial soil carried by the flow. All these elements came together and evolved until, around the sixteenth century, this inhospitable land was tamed by its inhabitants and adopted present structure and balance.

In the best places, usually along a strip running from the river a few miles (where the sandy soil is planted with the forests typical of the Landes region), this landscape offers an

incomparable vista of great undulating mounds, swelling like water one after another, with here and there a more heavily marked division created by a stream or *jalle*, a small retaining pond. When they look at the soil, visitors are invariably struck by the layer of white and gray pebbles blanketing the ground, lending the vinyards the appearance of a beach planted with vines.

The size of the pebbles varies from one place to another: huge and oval at Pauillac, in the center of Médoc, where they cover the ground almost uniformly; smaller and more irregular at Margaux, where they mingle with a layer of topsoil. These differences in appearance are not sufficient in themselves to justify the difference in taste between Margaux wines (reputed to be more refined and delicate) and Pauillacs (appreciated for their full flavor and power), but they play an intrinsic part in developing the outstanding quality of these vintages. In addition to favoring the ideal drainage, these also serve as heat accumulators in summer. With their feet constantly warm, a the vines bear grapes which ripen better and more evenly than elsewhere.

What lies beneath these stones, called *graves* in French? More *graves*! The top layer, generally eight to twelve inches deep, can sometimes extend as far as ten yards down. But it always lies over a denser subsoil of either marl (a mixture of clay and lime deposits into which the roots can easily penetrate), or clay which retain moisture and cool the vines, or chalky or sandy subsoils that are less rich, and which slightly diminish the vigor of a wine but enhance its finesse.

Vine are spaced more or less densely depending on the type of soil—the spectacular layer of pebbles on one of the best plots of Château Lafite (*left*) and their no less imposing presence in the vineyard of Château Smith-Haut-Lafite in the Bordeaux region of Pessac-Léognan (*above*)—as well as on climate and local growing methods. A glance at the photo on the left shows that the leading Médoc vineyards space the vines very densely—barely a meter apart, with the rows also fairly close. Here there are twice as many plants per acre as in numerous vineyards in southern Europe, where the lack of water makes it impossible to feed so many plants. High density is a key factor in quality, as it limits the number of bunches per plant and forces the roots to push deeper in order to find sustenance.

Along with Margaux, the Pauillac area —which covers just two villages—is certainly the most famous wine district of Médoc. Starting on the bank of the Gironde, it heads inland just a few miles, and, to the casual observer, is fairly uniform in appearance with gentle swells of rolling land, the soil evenly covered by large pebbles rounded over time, and vineyards and châteaus that vie with each other n lavishness and originality.

Each estate, called a *cru*, relies on this apparently identical soil to produce its wine. The uniformity is deceptive, however, for in fact subtle differences in the topsoil—and even more so in the subsoils—affect the wines' style. The three Pauillac *crus* awarded the most prestigious *premier cru* rating during the official classification in 1855 are near neighbors, and at first sight it seems hard to imagine what —apart from the appearance of the estate buildings might distinguish them.

Château Latour is furthest to the east, next to the vineyards of Saint-Julien, and its vines border the estuary, whereas Mouton and Lafite are further west and inland, not far from the vineyards of Saint-Estèphe. The proportion of stones is naturally greater along the river than elsewhere, and their size is also more impressive. If a visitor were to dig in the vicinity of the famous round tower that has come to symbolize the Latour estate, he or she would be surprised by the persistent presence of layers of pebbles, which are almost as dense several yards below ground as they are on the surface. Then the ground steadily turns into a rich, clayey subsoil, which recessitated the installation of artificial drainage in the nineteenth century. Benefiting from the mild and steady temperatures endowed by the broad river, Latour enjoys almost ideal soil and weather conditions. The vines never lack freshness thanks to the clay, which assures the roots a constantly stimulating environment, while the grapes may ripen early thanks to the heat of the stones in summer. Finally, the microclimate along the banks of the Gironde eliminates any risk of spring frosts and limits sharp variations in temperature: it is, therefore, not surprising that Château Latour is the most consistent of the Médoc *crus*, and that its style is often impressive in its depth and the density of its texture.

THE PUZZLE OF THE TERROIR

European wine-growers acquired this knowledge of their *terroir*—the combination of local soil and climate—very early on. Before the existence of geologists, many people working the vineyards had already realized that a given plot would produce better wine than its neighbor. During the Middle Ages, monks from the abbey of Cluny became the first to establish a hierarchy for a wine region. Mâcon, by

Above and *right*: With its extraordinary soil, climate, and location, Château Latour was already one of the most expensive Bordeaux vintages in the eighteenth century, alongside Margaux, Lafite and Haut-Brion. In 1790, the wine-loving former American ambassador to France, Thomas Jefferson, wrote to the owner of Latour on behalf of George Washington. "[I] know it is one of the best *crus* in the canton. I praised it thus to our President, General Washington, and he consequently charged me to ask you to be so kind as to supply him with twenty dozen bottles of your best wine for current service." *Following pages*: La Rochepot, in Hautes Côtes de Beaune, Burgundy. Located on the inland rise behind Côte de Beaune and Côte de Nuits, the Hautes Côtes vineyards are typical of plantations deeply rooted in local rural tradition.

dividing it into countless little plots of land which they classified according to their ability to yield either a divine nectar or a simple table wine to be drunk within the year.

Monks at the abbey of Cîteaux, founded in the late eleventh century, did even better on their surrounding vineyards in the Côte d'Or region. Cîteaux's twelfth-century holdings would turn any of today's large landowners green with envy, streching as they did from Clos Vougeot (now divided among more than fifty wine-growers!) as far as to Meursault and Pommard. The monks worked the soil and vines tirelessly, and knew better than anyone whether a given spot received more sunshine than elsewhere, and whether the grapes there ripened earlier, or were fleshier and tastier. This they demonstrated over time and through experience, that criteria other than the geological composition of the soil contributed to the construction of a great wine.

The bluffs of Burgundy that border the right bank of the Saône River rise fairly steeply from Dijon in the north down to Chalon, sixty miles to the south. Dominating the placid, fertile valley, they also mark the start of the impoverished, arid heights of the Massif Central. There is a striking contrast between the heavy rich soil that sticks to your shoes down in the valley, and the thin, chalky soil that emerges once the slope steepens, a difference which becomes yet more marked as the altitude of the hills slowly rises. At the bottom, the slope is gentle and the morning sun barely caresses the ground; halfway up, the summer sun shines down from morning to early evening, when it finally sinks behind the hills to the west. If a stubborn shower should drench the vines, no puddles form in the middle of the slope, for the rain immediately drains down to the bowels of the very porous soil. At the foot of the hill, in contrast, the subsoil is heavy and compact, like that of the plain, and water may stagnate.

The medieval monks were not unaware of all this. On the contrary, they knew better than anyone exactly where the heat was most intense in summer, or where their feet got muddy when they pruned the vines. The abbey's cellar-master and his team knew all the vineyard's secrets. They assessed the threats facing it, and they evaluated its strengths and weaknesses. They knew that, above a certain altitude, ripening occurred later and suffered too often from the rains and rigors of autumn prior to harvesting. Far from fitting the traditional image of tubby, red-faced monks, they were grave in their comportment and rarely drank the nectar they produced, for the order's draconian rules permitted just one pint of wine per week. Nevertheless, they were working in the process of discovering and glorifying the *terroir*, that subtle alchemy between plant, soil, and sky.

At one time or another, all wine-growers the world over have undertaken this quest for the perfect balance that characterizes a great *terroir*. It is quest that has become more urgent in vineyards where a

Right: Ancient presses in the abbey of Kloster Eberbach at Eltville, in Germany's Rheingau district. This type of traditional press dates back to the Roman era, and represents one of the surest ways to press the finest juice from grapes because it can be halted as soon as overly acid or oily components begin to flow: the grapes are placed in an oak hopper and then pressed by a plate lowered by a hand-turned screw. Similar presses are still used today in many regions (although powered by different means!), notably in Champagne. *Above*: This fourteenth-century illumination (taken from Shaw's *Dresses and Decorations of the Middle Ages*, vol. I) shows a monk sampling wine with a tasting cup in a cellar.

determination to produce wines that favor quality over quantity has surfaced only in recent decades. Nothing, indeed, is more crucial than knowing whether a famous variety of grape will be a winning transplant or will merely produce a wine with no vices but few virtues.

Agronomic researchers and technicians have sometimes favored certain parameters over others. In many New World vineyards, for instance, they long overlooked geological factors inorder to focus mainly on the effects of climate. A few years ago, the oenology department of the University of California at Davis divided the local vineyards into climatic zones based on average daily temperature on the one hand and rainfall on the other. Geological diversity may not be as marked in California as it is in Europe, whereas heat and rainfall vary significantly in the state from north to south and even more so from west to east, in the numerous folds between the coastline and the Sierra Nevada. Along the ocean, where the weather tends to be damp and cool, growers have often planted grape varieties which do well in the more rigorous European climates. German and Alsatian varieties such as Riesling and Gewürztraminer here yield original if ambitious wines that are richer and creamier, with fruity or flowery aromas that may appear exaggerated. Similarly, some of the best sparkling wines in California come from the state's coolest valleys, just as Champagne is, after Alsace, the most northerly wine-growing region in France.

Left: Clos Vougeot. *Above*: Clos Saint-Jacques in Gevrey-Chambertin.

Writer Antoine Blondin described a visit to Burgundy as follows: "The vineyard to which we had been invited by Roger Duchet —senator, mayor, and a former government minister—seemed somewhat sad beneath the thick clouds. And the famous villages we passed—Gevrey-Chambertin, Chambolle-Musigny, Vougeot, Vosne-Romanée, Volnay, Meursault—all seemed dully threatening. We had the impression we were visiting battlefields, where we would have to do battle with the Rugiens, the Brussanes, the Perrières, the Renardes, the Amoureuses, the Fremierts and Jarolières, the Cras, the Charmes, the Santenots du Milieu (and the just plain Santenots), all proud wines of first, indeed finest, growth." Blondin exited the battlefield glass in hand, victorious if somewhat befuddled (taken from *Ma Vie entre les lignes*).

As soon as this coastal climate is left behind, California presents a series of valleys, each drier and more continental than the last, with cold, sharp winters and summer temperatures that climb as high and quickly during the day as they drop at night. These are steep valleys, so that even during the most intense heatwaves the wind rolls down between the mountains to cool both grapes and inhabitants. The closer you get to the mountains, of course, the drier the climate becomes and the more marked the discrepancy in temperatures between winter and summer, day and night. Grapevines may be hardy, but there comes a point when they can no longer bear such conditions.

Starting in the 1950s, a handful of winemakers inspired by oenologist André Tchelistcheff realized the enormous potential of the Napa Valley. This welcoming valley north of

San Francisco was already a safe distance from the influence of the ocean while still free from the arid effects of the far-off mountains. It seemed certain that the land could produce better wines than those made in existing vineyards. The greatest European grape varieties were duly planted, and did well. Beaulieu Vineyards was the first Napa Valley estate to decide to give the great Bordeaux wines a run for their money, and its example was followed by many others.

Yet a quick glance by a casual visitor is enough to reveal how few similarities there are between Napa Valley's pleasant hills and Margaux's rippling fields, or between the sunny Californian summer and the harsh climate of Burgundy. The only thing lacking in California was a little water, which drip irrigation systems solved. Between the prestigious vineyard of Napa and Europe, each piece of the *terroir* jigsaw differs, and yet the whole puzzle comes together to present the vines with a similar picture: sun on the surface, heat on the ground, drainage and coolness in the subsoil.

TAMING THE VINE

While the soil-and-climate combination determines a wine's individual personality, the variety (or varieties) of grape constitutes the family of taste to which it will belong. The grower decides which variety of grape to plant, and from time immemorial people have grown two basic types, one designed to produce table grapes, the other to produce the fermented beverage called wine. Even if a few varieties can do double duty—Chasselas and some Muscat varieties, for instance—eating grapes and winemaking grapes belong to two completely different universes.

The reason is simple: in red wine, tannins and the other essential substances (apart from water and alcohol) come from the skin of the

Grapes are not the only things the Californians have borrowed from France. Many estates bear names with French-sounding names, such as *Au Bon Climat*, which seems to come straight from Burgundy (*above*). Nor is the phenomenon limited to California. Many new wine-producing countries also draw on exotic-sounding names, whether French, Italian or German. The world of wine has always been, by nature, fond of international exchanges. *Right*: A vineyard in Napa Valley, the heartland of quality California wines.

grape. And whatever the color of the wine, a variety of vine with small grapes will have a higher concentration of sugar than one with larger grapes. The sugar will become alcohol, the water will remain water. Therefore most of the good winemaking varieties are characterized by small grapes with thick skins. Larger, thinner-skinned varieties, on the other hand, obviously make the best table grapes.

Some forty species of grapevine are capable of producing wine. When, sometime around 1000 CE, Leif Ericsson discovered a land that would later be called Canada, the proud Viking was so impressed by the profusion of wild vines growing everywhere that he named it Vinland. Those vines belonged to a particular species known as *Vitis labrusca* (in Latin, *labrusca* means wild creeper). Even though some *Vitis labrusca* is still grown in the northeastern United States, this species has long given way—as have other, even more obscure species—to *Vitis vinifera*, which now exercises a virtual monopoly on world winemaking. And yet, the broad family of *Vitis vinifera* (literally "winemaking grapes") contains numerous offspring. It comes as no surprise to learn that this major branch of European (and later worldwide) agriculture has been subjected to close scrutiny from every angle by learned minds for centuries.

Agronomists started to specialize in the study of grape varieties at an early date, dubbing this science ampelography, from the Greek word for vine, *ampelos*. The earliest of ampelographers set out to describe every type of grape, from the size of the leaves to the way they grew and ripened to the soils and weather that suited them best. It was a task which was to occupy the entire lifetimes of countless ampelographers. The authoritative reference work on the subject, listing and describing all the known varieties of grapes, was compiled at the end of the nineteenth century by Pierre Viala and Victor Vermorel, two professors from the University of Montpellier, and runs to no fewer than seven volumes of 400 pages each!

With vines—as with other plants—hybridization is often the rule. This is all the more true as grapevines display a rare eagerness to mutate genetically. In the past, whenever a traveler discovered a variety praised by natives in a distant land, he would immediately return with several shoots to plant back home. Thus vineyards all over the world have sprung from the whims of voyagers who have returned home to cultivate their souvenirs. But imported varieties often behave quite differently in newly adopted lands—climate, soil and growing practices might trigger a mutation that would put a new face on the variety, and soon give it a different pedigree.

A variety such as the Pinot family, all descended from the same founding ancestor, now numbers at least 100 related members. Most are listed according to the color of the ripe

Pruning and training of vines are essential to their cultivation, because on the one hand they make it possible to control the productivity of each plant by limiting the number of bunches, and on the other they encourage the best exposure of the grapes to sun and heat. There are many different ways to train vines, some of them vertical (*top*, women tending vines in Graves in the nineteenth century) and others, more classically, horizontal (*above*, the method traditionally used in Médoc, where the plant is divided into two lateral shoots, illustrated here at different ages of the plant). *Right*: Cabernet Sauvignon grapes in Médoc.

grape—Pinot Noir (black), Pinot Gris or Grigio (gray), Pinot Blanc (white), and so on. But wine-growers' poetic instincts have also given some country cousins distinctly different names, such as Pinot Teinturier and Noirien, not to mention the German Bürgunders and Klevners, and the Swiss Savagnin Noir, all of which are blended into local vintages.

Wine-growers formerly developed their vineyards by burying a shoot from an adult plant, waiting until it took root, and only then cutting it from the parent, an age-old method known as provining or layering. Starting in the nineteenth century, wine-growers managed to select the finest plants on their estates, in order to turn them into the progenitors of the entire vineyard.

For centuries, vines in Europe were ungrafted, that is to say they grew on their own rootstock. The productive part of the plant was therefore directly affected by any soil-borne parasites. Thus in the latter half of the nineteenth century European vineyards found themselves waging a terrible battle against their most dreaded enemy, phylloxera.

The modest phylloxera aphid long remained unidentified, for it had coexisted with indigenous American varieties of vine without doing any visible damage. In 1860, when a few hundred American vines were imported into France, the parasite crossed the ocean and the shortened time of transatlantic voyages made it possible for it to survive the trip more or less intact. For five years, it multiplied discreetly in Provence and Languedoc without anyone noticing. But soon, wine-growers watched in horror as their vines lost their leaves, the grapes refused to ripen, and finally the vines themselves withered and dried up. By the time the vine died, its entire root system had been devoured by the parasite.

The disaster seemed as sudden as it was mysterious. In 1868, after a few years of diverse and divergent hypotheses, a professor at the University of Montpellier finally identified the culprit. But that did not slow the invader's advance. For nearly forty years, phylloxera ravaged French vineyards one after another, and methodically and mercilessly attacked all the other countries of western Europe. Even as this war was raging, another enemy surfaced—a fungus called "downy" mildew. It took four years to discover that mildew could be treated with an application of copper sulfate and lime called *bouillie bordelaise* (Bordeaux mixture). It was only on the eve of quite another war, in 1914, that phylloxera was ultimately vanquished. The American origins of the parasite had been discovered, along with the resistance of Ameri-

Working the vineyards has been considered one of the noblest of agricultural tasks since time immemorial, and many poets have celebrated it, such as Joachim du Bellay in the sixteenth century: "This vine so useful / of grapes so fertile / is ever faithful to its master. / And now that it hath flower'd well / Devote thyself and on it dwell / Thenot, thou self-same vintner. / And Bacchus, you, do what you should / that Thenot offer no complaint / of what he gets from such a plant. / And may my Anjou be endowed / everywhere with vine as good." Yet this lyrical symbiosis between plant and master has been sorely tried over the centuries, the worst affliction being that of phylloxera. *Above*: Infected vines in Médoc being ripped out in the early twentieth century. *Left*: A system used in Champagne to protect the vines.

can vines; by systematically grafting European varieties to American rootstocks, new vineyards were created that could henceforth hold out against the invader.

Although now rendered harmless, the phylloxera aphid was still present. And in a surprising "return to sender," it took advantage of the massive exportation of European plants to destinations such as California, Australia and New Zealand to launch an attack on vineyards there, previously thought to be safe. By the end of the nineteenth century, it is estimated that almost the entire Californian vine plantation had been grubbed up and replaced with resistant, grafted plants.

The phylloxera crisis altered vine cultivation permanently. First of all, it transformed into a science what had previously belonged to the sphere of tradition. This new area of research immediately showed itself highly exigent, on a scale consonant with the destruction wrought by the vineyard diseases of the nineteenth century. Throughout the twentieth century, agronomists and academics have conceived and oriented their work toward the constant goal of preventing a similar tragedy, not only for the vineyards but also for the eco-

nomy and social equilibrium of their respective countries. It is hardly surprising that over the decades their efforts, by overly protecting the plants, should frequently have led to insipid styles of wine.

In the late nineteenth and early twentieth century, agronomists shared Dr. Frankenstein's dream: they hoped to create a perfect plant. By crossbreeding a disease-resistant variety with another that ripened early, and by re-crossing the results with a third variety known for its abundant yield, then with a fourth reputed to produce a heavenly nectar, researchers thought they could produce a variety displaying all those qualities. But they suceeded only in creating hybrids which plunged wine culture into a sea of mediocrity more surely than all previous scourges had done. Fortunately, the perverse effects of such research began to be noticed in the 1950s, and hybrid varieties were slowly abandoned.

A different threat is more recent. In the second half of the twentieth century, agronomists created clones for every variety (or at least the most common types), making it possible to select the most attractive species by limiting random factors to a minimum. Although this research represents a major step in the history of vine cultivation, it was largely misapplied at first. Vine and wine alike fell victim to one of the principal evils of the final years of the second millennium: standardization. More or less everywhere, including the most prestigious vineyards, carefully selected clones were planted—the easiest to cultivate, the most productive and most resistant— in the great hope of escaping the absolute arbitrariness of the vegetable kingdom, thereby creating a risk-free (if adventure-free) vineyard.

A little later, it was realized that these magnificent clones had one drawback: although each plant produced more grapes, the wine it yielded displayed a serious lack of

Above: This nineteenth-century engraving shows the daily tasks carried out by wine-growers' wives in winter: pruning, training or, as here, bending vines on a trellis to force them in the desired direction. The method is the same today, although the shoots are now tied with wire instead of rush. In the past, the work of wine-producers in most regions was almost entirely agricultural, consisting of exhausting repetitive tasks such as tilling for men and pruning for women. On small estates, the actual winemaking was done in the simplest way possible; on larger ones, the job was entrusted to outsiders. It is only in recent decades that this second part of a wine-grower's role—which takes place in the cellar—has taken on a crucial importance everywhere.

THE WORLD OF VARIETALS

density, complexity and subtlety. The high-productivity approach, where "champion" grapes come off a production line overfed with chemical fertilizers, soon revealed its alarming limits. These limits were the same as the ones being encountered in industrially grown vegetables, intensively cultivated orchard fruit and—with even more drastic consequences—in battery-raised chickens and livestock fed on animal carcasses.

The wine of poets and artists has no need of such an industry. Sparked by a new generation of grape growers who are more idealistic than their parents, the clones used today are chosen not for their guaranteed productivity but for the quality of the wine they yield. Today there exist two types of vine cultivation—one highly productive, the other highly demanding—just as there exist two types of wine: those which are prefabricated and uniform, and those with a personality and soul all their own. It is up to the connoisseur to choose.

Topsoil, subsoil, climate, exposition, vine: the elements are all in place. Yet together they would make only a totally anonymous wine if two specific talents were not brought to the task. The most obvious of these skills lies in the wine-grower's hands and heart. A single-minded determination to produce "the greatest wine on earth" may change a good many things, transforming the ordinary into the complex, the parochial into the refined, the heavy into the exquisitely balanced.

Crucial as this talent is, there also exists another, similar one: the one contributed by the variety of grape. Through its ability to adapt—or not—to a given soil and climate, a given variety shapes the profile and personality of the wine. Just as a winemaker working on ten different estates would produce ten different wines, so each variety achieves a distinct expression in each vineyard. Production condi-

Above: Cabernet Sauvignon is the most famous variety of red grape in the world. Like its relative, Cabernet Franc, it was planted in the Bordeaux region at a very early date, mainly in Médoc and Graves, where it remains the principal variety on most estates. In the nineteenth century it was also planted in other areas, such as Provence and Tuscany (where it has long featured at the famous vineyard of Sassicaia). But the great international vogue for Cabernet Sauvignon began in the 1950s, when it arrived in Napa Valley and then moved throughout California and into Chile. The great vintage years for Cabernet Sauvignon—which means the great vintage years for Médoc—correspond with a sunny, fair autumn, the most recent examples being 1990 and 1996. A ripe Cabernet yields a dark red wine, rich in tannin and body, endowed with profound aromas of red berries.

tions are also enormously important—a plant overladen with bunches of a noble lineage which are picked before the grapes are perfectly ripe will obviously not yield the same wine as the same variety when harvested according to the rule book.

This ability of a variety to express itself differently according to soil and handling is not always immediately obvious to wine-growers and wine lovers. Both groups too often think that you need merely plant a famous variety of grape in a vineyard in order to produce a varietal wine displaying the finest features of that type.

This misconception is easy to understand. For centuries, the realm of grape varieties has been subject to a rigorous hierarchy. Early wine-growers did not classify grapes in terms of quality, but they knew which variety was the most disease-resistant, which would ripen the fastest, which would make their daily tasks easier. And then, at a very early date, by comparing wines produced by different varieties (and their market value!), they assessed the qualitative potential of each one.

Along with the Rhine Valley, the Mosel Valley has served as the cradle of German winemaking. The spectacularly steep slopes overlooking the tranquil river between Trier and Koblenz have been domesticated by people since the Roman era. Vines planted there have remained synonymous with exceptional quality century after century. For many years, these vineyards were also planted with a traditional local variety of grape, Elbling, now long forgotten. The extraordinary qualities of its soil and climate sufficed to guarantee the fame of the Mosel region and, in a historical Germany divided into numerous political entities each of which vaunted its own culture, people hardly though of changing what had become a habit.

The success of the Riesling variety, planted in the nearby Rheingau region from the late Middle Ages, nevertheless began to intrigue and then attract Mosel wine-growers. In the seventeenth century, they began to plant Riesling on their hillsides, and it took very well. In Rheingau, Riesling is able to produce thick wines that are wonderfully rich yet fresh. In Mosel, the variety underscores the natural finesse of wines produced in that area. Two different expressions, but both excellent. A variety that adapted so well to the semi-continental climate of western Germany soon won unanimous praise.

Sometimes, however, it takes a great leader to confirm —indeed, dictate—a given variety's supremacy. Pinot Noir, for instance, is the main variety used for red wines in Burgundy since the late Middle Ages. This eminently thoroughbred grape is able, when skilfully mastered, to produce wines with all the attraction of dazzling youth, expressing with joyful exuberance hints of raspberry, blackcurrant and blackberry, demonstrating on the palate a liveliness and dynamism worlds away from the rigid linearity of many wines. Furthermore, great Pinot Noirs age well, and connoisseurs marvel at the sovereign complexity of the range of flavors that Burgundies such as Charmbertin or Chambolle-Musigny are able to inspire after ten or fifteen years of aging.

Above: Riesling grapes. "Small, yellowish, and not very juicy; but it is one of the great grapes of the world," argued Alexis Lichine in his *New Encyclopedia of Wines and Spirits* (New York, 1978). Yet Riesling has not achieved the same worldwide success as its Burgundian rival, Chardonnay. It remains rooted to the soils of Alsace and Germany, notably the steep slopes of the Rheingau (*right*), which stretch a few dozen miles west of Mainz. The Rheingau has inspired poets such as Guillaume Apollinaire: "The Rhine is drunk where vines dress / In all the gold that trembling falls from night / Reflecting voices of a rattling death / While green-haired fairies chant a summer's sight." ("Nuit Rhénanes," *Alcools*).

Pinot Noir is nevertheless a demanding variety, often not very productive and highly sensitive to the vagaries of weather (and heaven knows that Burgundy is not very indulgent on that score). To top it all, this variety shows absolutely no mercy toward wine-growers who are not sufficiently rigorous. All wine connoisseurs—and, average drinkers perhaps even more so—have found themselves confronted on occasion with a Burgundy that lacks soul and color, whose aromas are fleeting and whose body is thin, undoubtedly the product of an overly abundant harvest of Pinot Noir, picked too early. So from the earliest times, Burgundian wine-growers have had to reconcile themselves to the fact that they married their destinies with a fickle variety.

In the Côte d'Or region, another red grape once competed with Pinot Noir, namely Gamay. Where Pinot Noir stand-offish at first, Gamay was immediately welcoming and friendly. Its vines were productive, and the grapes ripened quickly to give a wine with a deep ruby color. Gamay is more resistant than many varieties to disease and other scourges, and it makes life a lot easier for wine-growers. The grape has only one drawback: it insists on producing a wine in its own likeness—healthy, straightforward and fun, but hopelessly lacking the aristocratic elegance of its vineyard companion.

Between the demands of the one and the ease of the other, many wine-growers opted for simplicity. Hence in the fourteenth century Pinot Noir ran the risk of being totally eclipsed by Gamay's easy victories. It was the Duke of Burgundy himself, Philip the Bold, who put an end to this supremacy by issuing a decree forbidding the planting of Gamay on his territory, under penalty of heavy fines. And so this overly charming variety emigrated to the Beaujolais region which, though next to Côte d'Or, did not belong to the intransigent duke. Even then, the grape's emigration was only partial, since many Burgundian wine-growers continued to grow Gamay in secret. It retains a minority presence in the area even today.

Varieties took root all across Europe according to mood—their own or the wine-growers'. Some turned out to be natural conquerors, while others were awarded a realm on a silver platter. Gamay, for instance, received a triumphant welcome in its new home in the Beaujolais.

In other lands, the multiplication of independent states, combined with transportation difficulties, led to highly distinctive planting habits. In Italy, for example, Sangiovese—grown by the Etuscans—required time to take root, but once it had done so, in the early nineteenth century, it permanently and almost totally conquered the vineyards of Tuscany, notably producing the region's most famous wine, Chianti. Yet even in the last century, many wine-growers had doubts about the true qualitative potential of this variety, which was certainly honorable but a long way from superlative. There was no turning back, however, and Sangiovese is now indissociably linked to the region's vineyards. But as soon as you leave the Tuscan hills and the plains of Emilia-Romagna, its devotees become rarer and its empire peters out. The same fate befell another great Italian variety, Nebbiolo, which is limited to a single wine-growing region, the Piedmont. The reasons for Nebbiolo's inability to export itself, however, are precisely the opposite: whereas Sangiovese might appear to lack personality, Nebbiolo fairly oozes with it. With its thick skin and small grapes, it is one of the varieties richest in tannin, the woody substance contained in the skins and stems of grapes. Tannins give red wines their structure and endow them with the raspy character

Not all varieties of grape ripen in the same way and at the same time. A wine-grower's task includes deciding the date of optimum ripeness for each variety on the estate, and then organizing a coherent and efficient picking schedule. The ideal maturity of the grape can be determined by taking into account the steady decline in the grape's natural acidity and the steady rise in its sugar levels. Thus most grapes destined for dry white wines (like these bunches of Sauvignon, *left*) can be picked fairly early. In certain regions of southern France and in special weather conditions, some varieties are occasionally picked as early as the latter half of August, in order to retain the natural acidity in the wine. Conversely, grapes destined for sweet wines will be picked as late as possible, since sugar level is the key factor.

often noted by wine drinkers. Nebbiolo's acidity is startling; when tasting a Barolo, the greatest wine from Piedmont, drinkers are always struck by its wonderful, sudden associations of tannic strength and liveliness, between power and sleekness. But Nebbiolo manages to transcend this unique feature only in wines produced in its harsh, beloved hills of Piedmont. And even then not in all the hills, but only those facing due south, where the sun's rays are still strong in autumn, allowing the grapes to ripen slowly, lengthily, tardily. When other varieties have long since been picked, Nebbiolo requires still more patience. And should the fall turn cold and rainy, winegrowers know they will have to cross off the whole year, or least get used to the idea of producing a wine overly hard and acidic. It is easy to see why few people in the rest of the world are tempted to plant this variety—and yet, what character!

These selections and rejections, these slow invasions and lightning conquests have taken place in Europe over a period of centuries. Things were quite different when high-quality winemaking developed in the New World. Even though certain regions of America and the Antipodes have had major vineyards since the nineteenth century, these mainly grew robust, highly productive grape varieties. When, after the Second World War, a few ambitious enthusiasts decided to produce wines in California that might one day compete with the finest European vintages, they immediately realized that their vineyards would have to be rethought. The combination of American pragmatism

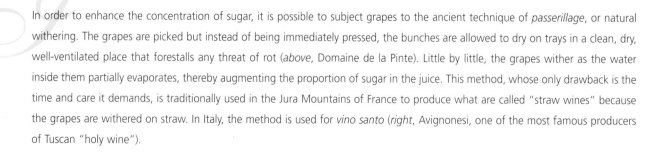

and the European experience of a handful of French-trained pioneers inspired the initial plantations. It was only natural that they should turn to the varieties which yielded the most famous wines, namely the red wines of Médoc and the white wines of Burgundy.

Cabernet Sauvignon is the name of the main variety of grape grown in Médoc (in association with others, notably Merlot). Cabernet Sauvignon is a hardy, easy-to-grow grape whose good nature does not prevent it from possessing absolutely dazzling qualitative potential. It is rich in tannin and color components, is capable of transmitting a bouquet of great nobility to the wine, and its range of berry-like aromas—redcurrants, blackcurrants, raspberries, wild strawberries—evolves over years of aging in the cellar into silky hints of cedar and Havana cigars. In short, Cabernet Sauvignon has few defects—except maybe that of ripening rather late and therefore suffering in poor autumn weather—while its qualities seem unparalleled. As soon as the first vines were planted in Napa Valley, their remarkable ability to adapt to conditions very different from those in Médoc thoroughly seduced the variety's American backers.

In Burgundy, meanwhile, white wines are made from a single variety, Chardonnay, which adapts wonderfully well to varying production conditions all along the lengthy, discontinuous strip of vineyards that make up the Burgundy wine-growing region. Chardonnay grapes in Chablis (in northern Burgundy, just a two-hour drive from Paris) yield wines of straightforward yet fine elegance, with

In order to enhance the concentration of sugar, it is possible to subject grapes to the ancient technique of *passerillage*, or natural withering. The grapes are picked but instead of being immediately pressed, the bunches are allowed to dry on trays in a clean, dry, well-ventilated place that forestalls any threat of rot (*above*, Domaine de la Pinte). Little by little, the grapes wither as the water inside them partially evaporates, thereby augmenting the proportion of sugar in the juice. This method, whose only drawback is the time and care it demands, is traditionally used in the Jura Mountains of France to produce what are called "straw wines" because the grapes are withered on straw. In Italy, the method is used for *vino santo* (*right*, Avignonesi, one of the most famous producers of Tuscan "holy wine").

pronounced mineral aromas, whereas in Meursault (100 miles further south), the wine is opulent and sumptuous, giving off bewitching scents of fresh butter and hazelnuts. Add to this that it is primarily responsible for the appetizing finesse of champagne, and it becomes clear that in its land of origin, Chardonnay has already demonstrated the many facets of its undisputed talent. So when it emigrated to California, its backers placed a great deal of hope in it. They were not disappointed.

Chardonnay enjoyed staggering growth in America, even more spectacular than that of Cabernet, because Anglo-American drinkers are fonder of white wines—usually drunk without food—than of red. In very different climes, and with suitably adapted winemaking methods, new-oak Chardonnays began displaying new qualities. Much more exuberant aromatically, rich and almost creamy in the mouth, their opulent, appetizing fragrances of butter, caramel, and hazelnut instantly appealed to drinkers. First planted in California in the 1950s, the Chardonnay vineyards have grown exponentially to become synonymous with all white wines with ambition.

Chardonnay's success, like that of Cabernet Sauvignon, has shot around the world—all the countries that have become interested in high quality wine more or less recently have begun to plant these two miracle varieties. In less than thirty years, Chardonnay and Cabernet have become stars in California, Chile, Argentina, Australia, South Africa, and New Zealand, not to mention Bulgaria, Italy (where they have also inspired very ambitious *vini de tavola*, or table wines) and even France, where both varieties have made startling inroads in the Languedoc region. This twin supremacy has reached the point where many consumers the world over associate these two names with high quality reds and whites, performing a role formerly played by the finest French appellations.

Today, the labels of many white wines from Burgundy now bear the word "Chardonnay" in more imposing letters than the appellation "Burgundy." American wine dealers, meanwhile, have launched the new concept of "ABC wines," aimed at all those who are weary of the ubiquitousness of the two varieties and who hope to discover something new. ABC stands for "Anything But Chardonnay/Cabernet...." Such is the price of success.

VINES THROUGH THE SEASONS

Once the stage has been set, this green drama is set to unfold. In antiquity, engravers and sculptors glorified the successive stages of work in the vineyards, at different seasons of the year. A thousand years later, medieval miniatures, tapestries, and frescoes celebrated the same tasks, carried out in conditions and with equipment that had barely changed from those of their forebears.

Tools have now evolved a great deal as the third millennium dawns, but the wine-grower's work remains basically the same: pruning the vines in winter, tilling the soil in spring, harvesting the grapes in autumn. This is the rhythm that paced the entire lives of generations of men and women, an immutable cycle that remains the same everywhere. The starting point, however, is reversed in the southern hemisphere, where the harvest takes place in March, at the end of the antipodean summer.

From the beginning of time, the natural world has always played its annual refrain of eternal rebirth. In the autumn, a few weeks after the harvest, the leaves of the vines take on mahogany fringes, then turn brown and finally fall. The bare vine is not dormant,

Right: Meursault and Meursault-Charmes (Premier Cru) from the Joseph Matrot estate.

Meursault, a village to the south of Beaune, at the tip of a long bluff running from Dijon straight down the Côte du Nuit and the Côte de Beaune, is the heartland of high-quality white wine production in Burgundy, along with the nearby villages of Chassagne and Puligny-Montrachet. The chalky soil of the area is perfectly suited to the Chardonnay grape, and the ideal southeastern exposure of Meursault's slopes gives its wines a richness and opulence that perfectly underscores delicious aromas of fresh butter and hazelnuts. Their style is markedly different from other great white Burgundies produced from the same grape, such as Chablis to the north, with its strongly mineral vivacity.

however. Its shoots continue to grow, giving the plant the strange appearance of a knotty gnome endowed with a series of skinny, ocher-colored arms. If the vine were allowed to grow in anarchic fashion, it would soon return to its original creeping habit, pushing countless shoots along the ground. Each stem would try to produce grapes, but the plant would not be able to satisfy all their demands—so some bunches would be healthy and ready to ripen, whereas most would be runty and incapable of developing. Winter pruning, then, is crucial in determining a vineyard's future.

Once the vines have reached maturity, after four years or more, pruning is designed primarily to keep the plant in its normal configuration, thereby insuring steady, regular production. When the vine is still young, however, the wine-grower will train its growth by allowing a given branch to develop while cutting back others, in order to arrive at the chosen shape. There exists numerous different pruning techniques, each designed to shape the vine differently. Over the centuries, wine-growers and agronomists have perfected their methods according to the lay of the land, the soil and climate, the variety of grape, and the requirements of production.

Thus from one region or tradition to another, vines may take on a very different appearance. Mediterranean vineyards adopt the goblet shape ("head pruning"), in which the branches seem to grow like a wine glass above the stem. In the "Guyot" method—the one most commonly used throughout the world—the young shoot is trained to grow at a right angle, extending parallel to the ground for several feet, guided by a wire. The supple grapevine will also adapt to other techniques, such as the "double Guyot" in which the shoots develop parallel to both sides of the stem. Then there is the "lyre" in which training is done vertically, giving the plant the attractive shape of the musical instrument.

Pruning is a chore for the cold winter months, and although it is now done with pneumatic clippers rather than a pruning knife, no machine can yet distinguish the good shoots from the others, so it is not much less onerous. For centuries, the wine-grower's wife followed behind her husband to gather the cut shoots into bundles which she would burn in the field on an ancient brazier. Today this task is divided more evenly between the sexes, but still it remains an exhausting one. As winter comes to an end, the vine is still naked, but has taken the shape it will keep until the grapes are picked—the shoots are attached to the wire trellis before the buds appear, develop, then loose their downy covering as the fruit emerges.

The months of March and especially April are the period of rebirth, when the vines waken and shakes itself from their apparent slumber. This is the time when wine-growers most fear a sharp frost which, on a single cold night in early spring, can drastically threaten

Left: Using a pruning knife (or today secateurs) to trim the vines is one of the wine-grower's key tasks in winter. Over the centuries, this rite has provided material for troubadours such as the clever Renaissance poet Clément Marot who humorously mocked the love songs rattled off by the poets of his day: "Change the tune, we've sung too oft of love / 'Tis naught but din, let's sing of pruning knives / Which vintners all grasp from above / that's how they trim their vines." By restricting the number of buds on the branch, vine-growers can regulate the productivity of their plants as well as their vigor and health. *Above*: Strips of wicker still used for binding (instead of wire) at Château le Pin in Pomerol, Bordeaux.

the potential harvest by literally scorching the tender buds.

After this perilous period, each bud will give birth initially to a tiny bunch. Each grain will slowly swell and then, in June, burst into flower. There is nothing spectacular about the flowering of the fine, small white blossoms, which are some of the vegetable kingdom's more modest creatures, and only survive a few days. No matter, because to wine-growers these flowers represent a liberation and a pro-

mise, namely of the harvest to come in one hundred days' time. In all traditional areas of vineyard culture, this moment is celebrated every year by a floral festival, which usually takes the form of a village festival but on Bordeaux estates can assume the trappings of a heraldic event.

Spring is also the time for tilling. Or rather it used to be, since this operation, designed to eliminate weeds that might choke the growth of the vines where also regenerating the soil by

Two depictions of work in French vineyards, half a millennium apart. *Above*: The medieval artist wanted to show every season of labor on vine and wine, from tilling (man with hoe, center), to pruning (with traditional curved blade, upper middle) to harvesting (picker with basket on back, center left). *Top right*: This photograph shows only one phase of work in the vineyard: burning the shoots removed during pruning, in the vineyard of Savigny-lès-Beaune in the Côte de Beaune region. *Bottom right*: Another view of the Savigny vines; the town of Beaune is located just a few miles south.

turning it and allowing it to breathe, has often been replaced by a simple dousing with chemical weedkiller. The modern technique is simple and spectacular—not a single weed invades the pristine rows of the vines—but does not allow the soil to recover its balance, so regular additions of fertilizer are needed to nourish the plants. It is a technique which indispensably forms part of the race for productivity that has gripped the world of wine in the past half century. Fortunately, more and more wine-growers are becoming aware of the dangers of this tendency, and there has been a return to tilling—in top-notch vineyards, at least—combined with a rejection of the systematic use of fertilizers, notably potassium. In vineyards as elsewhere, "organic" concerns are making great headway.

The organic approach also applies to the many treatments given to grapevines to protect them from the diseases and parasites that threaten them. This overdosing of medication is now being replaced by more measured treatment, carried out in early summer. It is also in summer that the vines' exuberant growth must sometimes be curbed. In leading vineyards, some owners now conduct what are called "green harvests" in July: to limit the output of grapes on each plant, a few bunches are removed, making it easier for the remaining bunches to grow in size and quality.

Obviously, an operation which entails deliberately sacrificing part of the crop would have seemed highly incongruous to previous generations of wine-growers, but it testifies to a phenomenal leap in productivity that has overtaken vineyard culture. The age-old dread of small harvests is now such a distant memory that people devise artificial techniques to reduce output.

Once the flowers have fallen, the grapes take definite shape, swelling quickly and starting to ripen by the month of July. The ripening process is lengthy, and continues throughout the summer. The green grapes will grow, take on a handsome blackish or golden sheen, then swell with sugar. Soon the time for picking will come—the magic moment when the fruit will be transformed into wine is at hand. And thereby hangs another tale.

*I*n the French countryside, wine is drunk at every age. This 1955 photograph, taken in Brillac, Charentes, shows two schoolboys tasting grape juice as it runs from the press, even before the must has begun to ferment. Adults would probably prefer to wait a few days, as Ugolin suggests in Marcel Pagnol's novel *Jean de Florette*: "'Hello, neighbor! So the grapes have been picked?' —'That's right, Monsieur Jean! The wine is drawn, it just needs drinking. Not much of it, but at least it's strong. I've brought you two bottles. Not yet ready, of course, but it's already good!'" *Following pages*: Drawing wine from the barrel (*left*) and tending casks in the cellar (*right*).

From
Grape
to
Wine

Nothing seems more timeless than the sight of an army of pickers cutting grapes on a fine summer evening. The mere description of such scenes immediately stirs the collective imagination, nourished since the Middle Ages by artists' painted, drawn and embroidered images. In illuminated manuscripts such as the *Très Riches Heures du Duc de Berry*, in Italian frescoes, or in the complex, masterly paintings of Flemish masters, it was the labor of men and women during the grape harvest—more than any other agricultural activity—that came to symbolize the life and devoutly respected moral values of the era.

Collecting "the fruit of the harvest" was a moment of liberation for western societies, a moment when the year's humble and laborious efforts were rewarded, a moment when work was gave way to celebration, joyous and peaceful. In short, these were special days around which the year and the seasons were orchestrated, until they became practically synonymous with autumn.

HARVEST DAYS

Every peasant took part in this work, which involved the entire wine-growing community. Women and children squatted beneath or leaned over the densely planted vines, advancing either in ordered rows or, to the contrary, "in a crush", (the traditional method in southern vineyards. They cut the stems which held the bunches of grapes with the help of a small blade not unlike a pruning knife, still in existence today. Occasionally, artists would depict the scene without any tools, as though the plant dropped its ripe fruit straight into humankind's outstretched hands.

The pickers—mostly women and children—would then place the bunches in small wicker baskets, or sometimes wooden buckets. These were never very large, since for over seven hundred years growers have known from experience that the quality of the wine depends on limiting the time it takes the grapes to get to the cellar and on preventing a heavy weight of bunches from prematurely bruising the grapes. Once a bucket was full, it would be taken to the men, who carried larger baskets—made of wooden staves bound with hemp—strapped to their backs. In extensive vineyards, the men would take their load to a cart pulled by a mule or cow, which would then transport the grapes to the place where the wine was made. Usually, however, the wine press and fermenting vat were set outdoors near the vines themselves, where the men would empty the baskets directly simply by leaning over.

This timeless image of the grape harvest has changed very little over the centuries. Similar baskets are still used today in many vineyards in Alsace and Germany, the original wood having been replaced by plastic. Grape-picking remains a village, or sometimes family, affair. In vineyards throughout the world, people work together and sometimes dance together. Here as elsewhere, however, the need to modernize suddenly became a necessity to many wine-growers. Tractors were soon easing the pickers' task. Trays were replaced by enormous dumpsters, which reduced the number of return trips necessary but also ignored the

Right: This Italian Renaissance fresco depicting grape-picking and winemaking at Castello del Buonconsiglio in the Trentino region shows in perfect detail the methods used throughout Europe in the Middle Ages (and right up to the nineteenth century). Women and children pick the bunches, which men then carry in little wooden baskets to the traditional press. Two men turn a bar which operates a screw, progressively lowering a beam that forces a crate onto the grapes, the juice running from a spout into a wooden cask. *Above*: As for red wine, this detail from a tapestry (Abbaye de Cluny, c. 1500) depicts whole bunches of grapes being trodden underfoot, a method which, without being the most hygienic, still remains the best way to release the finest juices and allow them to macerate in the skins.

traditional care taken to avoid crushing the grapes and triggering premature oxidation of the juice. (But since modernization often creates as many new needs as it eliminates, oenologists rapidly suggested adding anti-oxidant agents to dumpsters loaded to the brim with grapes practically transformed into jam already.)

Finally, in the 1970s, a number of manufacturers specializing in farm vehicles invented a machine that would totally revolutionize the image and practice of grape-picking in the twentieth century. The harvesting machine resembles a tractor on huge wheels, able to straddle a row of plants. The vines between the wheels are shaken by straps until the vibrations make the bunches fall. A vacuum then sucks up the fruit, along with—when the machine is not properly calibrated—leaves, pebbles and sometimes field mice. Several acres of vines may thus be gobbled up in a matter of hours, whereas a team of pickers would take several days to do the same work.

This invention created new requirements, however. Since it is obviously not suited to steep terrain, many hillside vineyards where access was difficult were abandoned, to be replanted on flat land. Mechanization was thereby facilitated, but considerations of soil and climate were disregarded. And, the machine treats the vines roughly, shortening their lifespan. Vineyards must therefore be replanted more often, every twenty to thirty years. And when you take into account the fact that vines

Evocative images of bunches of ripe, grapes busting with juice (*right*, Syrah grapes in Côte Rôtie), combined with the powerful symbolism of the harvest, have long inspired artists. This late sixteenth-century scene painted by Bassano Gerolamo (*above*) finds a perfect commentary in a poem by Rémi Belleau (1528–1577), written at about the same time: "Girls, boys, with baskets full / use all your might to haul / the dark-skinned grapes / with arms and backs / and Heave! them all into the vats. / Then feet of naked men may go / and tread them till from bunches flow / a new seed sure to grow. / To this good God let all now raise/ a hymn of harvest praise / And honor Him from all around / Let every place resound."

overproduce in their early years, and that it takes a good dozen years for them to begin to yield their best fruit, the limitations imposed by such practices soon become all too apparent.

So mechanical grape-picking was not destined or able to triumph everywhere. In some countries, moreover, maintaining an army of pickers every year represents a considerably less costly investment than the purchase of one of these expensive machines. At the other end of the financial scale, meanwhile, a good number of vineyards and wine-growers of noble pedigree have resisted the temptation to resort to the easy path, either because the terrain of their estates did not lend itself to such equipment, or because they felt it did not accord with the qualitative criteria they wished to respect in their work.

Indeed, the grape harvest undoubtedly represents the most crucial phase for anyone wishing to produce a great wine. When the fruit is ripe, it must be picked. Yet, despite the biblical simplicity of the idea, it is not so easy in practice. In the northern hemisphere, grapes reach a perfect most balance of ripeness sometime between late summer and early autumn. At this elusive moment, there will come a point when the grapes are saturated with sugar (which is converted into alcohol during fermentation), and when the tannin and other precious substances found in the skins will have become more concentrated and matured in their turn; but at the same time, the grapes still retain enough natural acidity to bring life and freshness to the wine.

Alas, many fine grape-growing regions are also characterized by a swift deterioration in weather conditions at the end of summer. This is particularly true in western Europe, from the valleys of the Rhine and Mosel to the furrows of Médoc, from the slopes of Burgundy to the hillsides of Piedmont. Hence the mortal sin most common among wine-growers in these regions is that of impatience.

In theory, grapevines follow a virtually unchanging cycle of growth, known and observed for centuries—down to its minutest details—by agronomists and vine-growers alike. Country wisdom maintains that the ideal date to begin picking is 100 days after the vines flower in spring. In fact, weather conditions during any given summer obviously have a considerable influence on this cosmic clock, putting it ahead or behind. Furthermore, not all varieties of grape ripen at the same rate. Some grapes are notable for their precociousness, and are ready to be harvested by late August; other varieties, on the contrary, take much longer to ripen, remaining imperturbably green until early October. In the intervening weeks a nerve-wracking comedy is played out every year, at the end of which growers hope they will not regret having waited too long or, much more commonly, having been overly hasty.

For centuries, wine-growers have been gripped by the ancestral fear of a lost harvest, ruined by the weather's sudden changes in mood. They know that the point at which their vines are laden with grapes is also the point at which they are most vulnerable. A brief hailstorm, not uncommon in late August, can destroy an entire harvest in a matter of minutes. Rain plays a more ambivalent role: an isolated, late-summer storm two or three weeks prior to picking will provide the plant and its fruit with a welcome bonus of nourishment, so prolonging its quest for ideal ripeness. In some southern regions—and occasionally even in northern vineyards during unusual years—summer drought may halt the ripening of the grapes. Like an undernourished child, the parched fruit refuses to open no matter how intense the sunshine spurring it. On the other hand, a shower just prior to picking brings no good whatsoever: the grapes swell with water they cannot assimilate, and the elements that make up a good wine—sugar, tannins, and

Right: The end of a day's picking in Champagne in the 1950s. As the nineteenth-century poet José Maria de Heredia wrote in *Les Trophées*: "The weary pickers, having broken their lines / Set voices ringing on evening air / To the press, in choir, march women fair / Mixing their songs with calls and signs." Note the modest size of the wooden crates that hold the grapes headed for the press; this prevents the grapes at the bottom from being crushed by those on top, and thereby spoiling before they are pressed. Unfortunately, the use of dumpsters is increasingly widespread in many vineyards, at the certain cost of quality.

acidity—do not have to the time to increase proportionately. They will merely be diluted in the added water, which means that the wine will suffer in strength, body, and balance.

What is to be done when rains arrive in the first two weeks of September? Wait until the process of ripening is launched afresh, its sails swelled with this new gust of growth? Certainly not, if the grapes are destined to make a dry white wine. From late summer onwards, the acidity of the grape is in steady decline, and is this component that is crucial to most of these dry white wines, whose buoyant vivacity is too important to be allowed to flag. For red wines, the answer may be different, however, and every year quality wine-growers across the globe prove that risk-taking is an integral part of their trade. Obviously, simple logic would suggest remaining patient, and waiting for the grapes to assimilaty this water and continue their course towards ripening and concentrating their essential sugars. But this tactic will work only if the rains stop, the grapes dry out, and a relatively fine Indian summer arrives.

Warm, damp weather, meanwhile, threatens to trigger rot. The tiny fungus spreads like a wildfire from one bunch to the next, soon contaminating the entire plant, and the danger is all the greater when the vines are heavy with grapes. At this point, the only effective defense against such attacks—the use of chemical products being of course forbidden so close to the harvest—is to have the bunches spaced sufficiently far apart. Growers who have taken the precaution of safe-guarding their production by thinning the grapes now reap an added benefit: sometimes nature *does* reward personal merit.

And sometimes not. In some autumns, the weather remains incessantly wet, with leaden days offering only yet more low, gray clouds that unleash icy, persistant showers. Clearly, such conditions do nothing to improve the quality of the grapes. They will not ripen any further, the diluting effect will increase, and the risk of rot will intensify. The only thing to be done is to limit the damage by harvesting right away.

In all these situations, whether the year looked highly promising or merely ordinary, it soon becomes apparent that there may be major differences in quality from one bunch to another, indeed from one grape to another. Increasingly, wine-growers with the highest standards are introducing draconian sorting techniques, either by asking the pickers to weed out mercilessly any bunches that have started to rot, ot that by contrast contain grapes that are still green, or by setting up sorting tables at the edge of the vineyard or in front of the cellar. Here others will cast a connoisseur's eye over the harvest, separating the wheat from the chaff. Constant vigilance and an incompromissing will: these are the two factors on which the quality of a wine depends.

GOLDEN HARVEST IN SAUTERNES

There may nevertheless be something rotten in the state of great wines—something that gives

Left: Harvested grapes arriving at the hopper at Château Haut-Brion, in the Pessac-Léognan wine region of Bordeaux. After having been selected first on the vine, then sorted on a conveyor belt, the grapes proceed to a stalk-removing crusher which eliminates the stems, then tumble into the hopper which takes them to the press and the vats. *Above*: A Chilean wine-grower with his harvest after a day's picking: an image recalling Lamartine's classic lines: "Listen to the harvest call, the press at work in nearby shed / See the stony barnward path bloodied by the grapes so red." *Following pages*: A harvest scene. Note the use of plastic baskets, a modern version of the wooden ones used in the Middle Ages. Apart from the materials, the work of harvesting is carried out in exactly the same way as five hundred years ago.

delight to both growers and wine lovers. Of all the many fungi that devour the skin of grapes during their growing cycle, there is one that does so with inimitable panache. Oenologists call it *Botrytis cinerea*; wine connoisseurs familiar with its beneficial effects simply "noble rot."

If the truth be told, Botrytis behaves nobly only in certain circumstances. Most of the time, and with most varieties (especially those used in red wines), it is one of those minor evils that afflict all vineyards. Yet once autumn has arrived, in highly specific places and climactic conditions, Botrytis may transcend its usual role of preventing grapes from ripening peacefully and become the catalyst for the alchemy of great dessert wines.

As has already been mentioned, a ripening grape steadily loses its acidity and gains in concentrated sugar. The simplest way to make a sweet wine is therefore to wait until the grapes wither on the vine (or on trays, after being picked; both are natural techniques of dessication, called *passerillage* in French). Botrytis completes this process of concentration by practically dissolving the skin of the grape, leaving only the flesh and sugar to be pressed.

All the regions where Botrytis flourishes share the common feature of being bordered by cool streams or rivers. In the mild autumn weather, the contrast between warm air temperatures and the cool water creates morning mists that encourage the growth of the fungus. So every year, this phenomenon finds a welcome setting, unchanged for centuries, along the small streams flowing down to the valleys of the Mosel, the Rhine, the Loire and the Garonne.

Set in gentle countryside on the banks of the Garonne River, some 25 miles southeast of Bordeaux, Langon is a bustling market town which modestly conceals its role as capital of one of the greatest—and, thanks to its richness, thickness and longevity, certainly one of the most original—wines in the world: Sauternes. The vineyards stretch all around, along the Garonne down by Barsac, and further inland on the gentle swells of Bommes and Sauternes itself. The most widely planted grape variety in the region is Sémillon. Used in the Bordeaux region to produce dry wines which age, acquiring remarkable charm and aromas of honey and honeysuckle, this white grape above all adapts perfectly to the arrival of Botrytis. The fungus spreads gradually and unevenly, however, from one plant to another, and from one plot to another.

Wine-growers and their armies of pickers must therefore go through the vines again and again, week after week, assessing in each row

Right: The picker's role becomes even more crucial when selecting grapes for late harvesting, as here at Château d'Arche in Sauternes. On every plant, some bunches will have reached a perfect stage of "noble rot" and must be picked, while others are only partly ready and must wait. Still others may not yet have been attacked by Botrytis but could deteriorate if not picked immediately. The man or woman who cuts the bunches must therefore judge on sight. The skins of grapes affected by noble rot practically turn to dust and look almost like raisins (*above*, grapes harvested at Château Rieussec). *Following pages*: An aerial view of the most famous Sauternes estate, Château d'Yquem, whose vineyard stretches across rolling, magnificently exposed waves of gravelly soil.

the grapes to be picked, and those that need to wait a little longer, in a painstaking selection procedure known as *le tri*. In some years, a few meticulous estates will make as many as five or six selections, extending from early September into the month of November.

In Germany, with its *Eiswein* ("ice wine"), in Alsace with its late harvest or selection of noble grapes, and in the Loire Valley with its Vouvrays, Bonnezeaux and Quarts-de-Chaumes growers may sometimes wait as late as December. Naturally, such harvests are costly and enormously risky—who can be confident the skies will smile upon them throughout an entire autumn?

THE MIRACLE OF FERMENTATION

For every grape, whatever its variety, or geographical origin, and whatever the type of wine it is designed to yield, the moment of picking represents the end of one cycle and the start of another, namely the astonishing biochemical adventure which will convert the fruit's sugar into alcohol and transform many other substances found in the juice or skin —or indeed the stem—into the essential ingredients of wine. This transformation is largely natural; humans merely guide and control it to insure its quality. Winemaking techniques have of course been extensively modernized and refined ever since the fourteenth century, attaining a veritable explosion of scientific advances during the last half-century. They are nevertheless based on prin-

ciples described and put in place hundreds of years ago. To come across them in a setting as yet untouched, where wine appears to be made in a way unchanged for one or two centuries is to shed a nostalgic but impressive light on the enduring nature of oenological principles.

The heart of port wine beats in Pinhao, a village on the banks of the Douro River, which cuts steep, wild valleys all the way to Porto and the Atlantic Ocean some sixty miles downstream. Yet here the river, tamed by a series of dams, is already as wide as the mouth of the Seine. Above the village of Pinhao climb the terraced vineyards of the best *quintas*, the Portuguese name for wine estates. These *quintas* constitute one of the two major centers of port wine, the other being situated at Vila Nova de Gaia, in the docks on the outskirts of the city of Porto itself, Lisbon's great rival. In the dark, ancient cellars of Vila Nova the wine that was harvested and fermented in the valley of the Douro ages slowly. Far from echoing the magnificence of châteaus in Bordeaux, a *quinta* looks just like what it is: a combination of a large Portuguese farmhouse and a nineteenth-century summer house (or hunting lodge) for noble families.

For many years, coming here was a veritable expedition. Owners who made their summer quarters here sailed up the capricious river in boats or, beginning in the late nineteenth century, rented a first class carriage in the train that snaked its way up the banks of the Douro, terminating at Pinhao. The wine then returned down the river on large barges, ending its journey in the cellars on the shores of the Atlantic. Up until the early 1960s, some *quintas* could

Above: Not all the grapes on a bunch are attacked by "noble rot" to an equal extent, as seen on this cluster from Château Sudiraut in Sauternes. First the rot invades a few grapes, then it spreads to the rest of bunch over a period of days. At picking time, the stage of Botrytis advance must be carefully assessed. *Right*: Quinta de Noval surrounded by terraced vineyards on slopes overlooking the august Douro River, some 100 miles from its mouth at Porto. The soil of this immense valley is completely composed of schist, so only vines—and, to a lesser extent, olive trees—can take lasting root here. The entire right bank, facing due south, is covered with vines to an altitude of 1,000 feet, the left bank being planted with vines only on the well-exposed slopes of adjacent valleys.

be reached only by river. And it was to be another thirty years before a highway was to halve
the travel time by car, which had taken over
three hours to cover a mere 100 miles.

For many years, this somberly beautiful
and grandiose land long managed to remain
rooted in another time. As the second millennium draws to a close, a new generation of
international proprietors has of course arrived,
accelerating the modernization of the landscape, of attitudes, and of working habits, but
you can still find *quintas* where time almost
seems to have stood still. Here people celebrate
the harvest period and the birth of a new wine
with the same peasant self-abnegation and
sometimes secret fatalism that marked this key
moment of the year in all the grand vineyards
of Europe in the nineteenth century.

As morning dawns in Quinta do Roriz on a
day in early September, the picking gets
underway while the sun is still hidden behind
the tall hills framing the vineyard. Thirty or so
pickers from the same up-country village
silently make their way toward the vineyards
that climb up from the river to the summit of
the steep hills, three hundred yards above. The
motley crew offers a full range of local charac-
ters from the depth of the country, from an old
lady dressed in black, dry and hard as the
vines, to a teenager in a brightly colored tee-
shirt. They come here every year; in the past,
the work was done by travelling gipsies, who
were valued for the care and quality of their
labor, but who in the end proved too expensive. So the team hands itself up toward a plot
that crests the highest terraces, and sets about
its work. Although wicker baskets have been
replaced by plastic buckets, the technique has
not changed for centuries. The bucket is carried to a cart, now pulled by a tractor; there
the grapes remain for several hours, in full
sun, until the cart is full enough to be taken to
the cellar. The tractor makes only two return
trips per day.

Heat is not good for grapes about to be
made into wine, since fermentation temperature is one of the key factors in determining
the quality of the wine. But it matters little
here, because the winemakers of old were careful to eliminate this problem by giving the
grapes time to cool down again. After a short
time in a primitive rocking called a wine-
press—in fact, a kind of beater that lightly
tears the skins to allow the juice to begin to
flow—the grapes fall into the *lagars*. These
large stone troughs, several centuries old, less
than three feet deep, and composed of wide
slabs, are a source of immense pride to their
owners. As an indication of the care devoted to
winemaking here from earliest times, *lagars*
are made of granite, a rock of which not one
ounce occurs naturally in the region. Roughly
one *lagar* is filled per day; the grapes are simply spread across the entire surface, to a depth
of about a foot and a half. There they await
the return of the pickers, after five o'clock in
the afternoon, when they will be trodden
underfoot.

These rudimentary techniques represent
the fundamental basis of the way all red wines
are made. Whether roughly crushed by the
harvesters' feet or by a machine with a turning
screw, the goal is the same: to enable the
grapes to release their juice and sugars. The
juice will ferment naturally in the open air, as
for that matter would the unpasteurized juice
of any fruit left in similar conditions. This
"continuous miracle" has been described by
observers of the agricultural and culinary
worlds for thousands of years; nor is the result
particularly miraculous in most cases, because
many fermented foodstuffs become unfit for
consumption. The exact explanation for the
process only emerged once people were able to
examine infinitely small objects, as the causes
of fermentation are microscopic: it is the result
from the action of the highly specific microor-
ganisms known as yeasts. Yeast is another fun-

All port wine is produced in the same way, by being fortified, which means that fermentation is brought to a sudden halt by the addition of alcohol. A significant part of the residual sugar therefore remains unfermented, even as the alcoholic content of the wine is notably increased. There are several varieties of port, divided into two major families. One of them, tawny port, is the result of slow, controlled oxidation of the wine through several years of aging in barrels, giving it an orange or mahogany color and aromas of leather, nuts or orange peel. Tawnies may be barrel-aged for ten, twenty or forty years, or they may correspond to a specific vin-tage year called *colheita*. *Left*: An interior view of the firm of Ramos Pinto, one of the great specialists in tawny port.

gus, although this time single-celled, making it much smaller than Botrytis and friendlishly more common. It is found absolutely everywhere: in kitchens, on food, in fruit, in trees and plants, and of course in cellars. Yeast comes in countless varieties. Some live in families in the same place for centuries, regenerating themselves every year, happily decamping from an abandoned building to a new one. This discreet player in the game of winemaking is not lacking in either voracity or self-sacrifice. Focusing its insatiable appetite on mushy grapes—called must—it will progressively transform the sugars into alcohol, releasing waves of carbon dioxide in the process. Each yeast cell will die from exhaustion in a matter of hours, to fall to the bottom in the form of dregs, or lees.

The ancient cellar in Pinhao represents an incomparable museum of fermentation yeasts. The broad shape of the *lagar* and the very gentle method of pressing provide for a highly propitious encounter between fungus and must. The pickers form two rows—adults in front and teenagers behind—with everyone standing side-by-side, one arm on a neighbor's shoulder and the second arm around another's waist. Then they crush the grapes underfoot, all pretending to climb an imaginary staircase together, co-ordinated by a solemn-faced leader chanting "one, two." This goes on for four hours, interrupted only by a brief break for a small glass of alcohol. As the evening wears on, the treaders begin to sing a little louder and have fun, until the signal for release is given as they all sing the "Song of Freedom," at which they scatter out across the *lagar*, still trending methodically but now in every direction and on their own. This ecstatic and good-natured ritual, full of joy despite the rigors of a fifteen-hour work day, proves to be amazingly efficient. The continuous human treading presses the grapes and flesh, producing a juice instantaneously

macerated in the pigments and tannins contained in the skins. Energetic though it may be, this type of extraction is considerably gentler than all known mechanical methods of punching and pressing.

The juice is already colored, becoming incredibly black in a matter of hours. It will ferment all night, embarking on the adventure that will transform it into port.

This method of producing red wine is specific to port, and all the more so because the very next day the wine will be fortified, a highly specific operation performed on only a few wines, such as Banyuls and Rivesaltes in France. Fortifying a wine consists of the sudden addition of a dose of strong grape alcohol, which halts fermentation by choking off the action of the yeast. Drowned in alcohol, the unfortunate yeast cells perish before they have converted all the sugar in the fruit. Wines made this way are therefore high in alcohol content—16 to 18 per cent by volume—while retaining a high and completely natural proportion of sugar. Apart from the fortifying process, however, the winemaking methods used in this *quinta*, traditional and particular though they are, are based on absolutely universal principles.

THE PRINCIPLES OF VINIFICATION

The first trick, as we have seen, consists of bringing grape juice into contact with the yeasts that trigger fermentation.

The second entails monitoring the fermentation to prevent it from going awry. In particular, the rise in temperature of the must (naturally provoked by the fermentation process) should not exceed certain limits, or else the wine will have an unpleasant taste; conversely, an excessively low temperature will not draw all the desired aromas and tannins from the must. Thus two major—and

The other family of port is known as "vintage." With its deep ruby color and captivating bouquet of dark fruit (which over the years will mature into complex fragrances of tobacco, leather or cedarwood), vintage port is an exceptional wine that can age for decades, like the finest Bordeaux wines. It is always made from the best part of the harvest and is produced only in good years, barely two or three each decade (and bearing no relation to great vintage years in France, since 1960, 1966, 1972 and 1977 were poor years in Bordeaux, but great years for port). Unlike tawnies, vintage port is not oxidized—the wine is removed from the barrels after only one or two years, then aged in the bottle. *Right*: Vintage port from one of today's finest producers, Fonseca.

incontrovertible—advances made by modern oenology have been strict temperature monitoring and an ability quickly to cool (or heat) the must if necessary. In the past, as a desperate measure, winemakers were sometimes known to toss chunks of ice into a vat that had overheated. These days, a simple switch will send water into tubes coiling around the stainless-steel vat.

The third principle pertains solely to red wines: the must has to macerate for a sufficiently long time in the crushed skins (or even with the stems) in order to acquire a color that is red, purple or even black, and above all to absorb the various substances contained in them, primarily tannins. With white wines, on the contrary, the chief concern is to retain as much of the fruit's freshness and finesse as possible—thus the grapes are swiftly pressed and the juice is not left in contact with the must.

The fourth principle, finally, entails obtaining a wine that corresponds to the quality or style expected of soil, climate and the reputation of the vintage. This final factor explains, if not excuses, the innumerable techniques employed throughout the world in following the first three rules. Furthermore, the god (or demon) of winemakers has provided them with a few little recipes designed to put a better face on wines that needed a helping hand. In the early nineteenth century, a French chemist by the name of Jean-Antoine Chaptal—also Minister of the Interior and founder of the Chambers of Commerce—published a winemaking treatise that laid the true foundations of modern oenology. Even though he castigated "the lack of

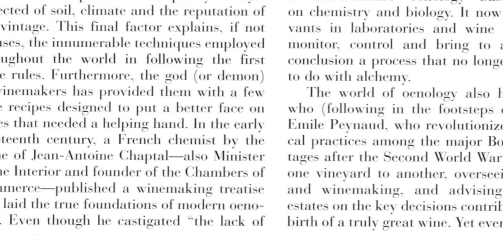

care [of some] vine-growers, [and their] blindly routine methods in ignorance or forgetfulness of the laws of nature, and the preference they give to varieties most abundant in coarse sugars rather than to those that produce wines of better quality," Chaptal nevertheless came to the aid of wines of weaker constitution by suggesting a technique that became a huge success: just add sugar to a vat in fermentation, and the alcoholic strength of the wine will be increased. Now known as chaptalization, this technique is extensively used throughout the world—and not only the world of modest wines—but nevertheless remains a last resort. It improves the alcoholic content, endowing none of the other virtues that constitute true quality in a wine.

The skills and techniques of winemaking were for many years the product of local or family tradition, handed down orally from father to son, without any real attempt to understand the underlying principles. In the past century, however, winemaking has become a science—oenology—based primarily on chemistry and biology. It now has its servants in laboratories and wine estates who monitor, control and bring to a successful conclusion a process that no longer has much to do with alchemy.

The world of oenology also has its stars who (following in the footsteps of Professor Emile Peynaud, who revolutionized oenological practices among the major Bordeaux vintages after the Second World War), race from one vineyard to another, overseeing harvests and winemaking, and advising the finest estates on the key decisions contributing to the birth of a truly great wine. Yet everyone knows

No one has celebrated the power of young wine better than sixteenth-century poet Pierre de Ronsard: "In September the tuns in Anjou are seen /to boil with frothy young wine / growling, hot-headed and ever so keen / to leap from its bung when inclin'd. / Fiery, impatient, no rest will it know / from swelling and fuming; to peace will not hark / 'til winter's cold breath tames its strength with a blow /and bars its pow'r in a prison of bark." *Right*: Racking wine from a vat in Bordeaux. *Above*: The vats where wine ferments until winter, when it is placed in an oak cask. *Following pages*: A vineyard at Cuis, in the Côte des Blancs region of Champagne.

that their role remains limited. Wines may be ruined, alas, by careless winemakers even though made from fine, ripe and concentrated grapes, but oenology will never produce a divine nectar from poor-quality grapes. When it comes to wine, everything depends on the grape. But when it comes to *great* wine, only human genius knows how to tease out its quintessence.

CHAMPAGNE, OR THE QUINTESSENCE OF HUMAN LABOR

To those expecting signs of sybaritic indulgence, the Champagne region offers very few obvious signs of the luxury, sophistication and celebration that its wine has come to symbolize throughout the world for centuries. True, visitors may note a certain grandeur in a few splendid buildings in the regional capital, as well as in the series of impressive facades along the Avenue de Champagne in Épernay (the third largest city in the *département* of the Marne, and the true heart of the Champagne

vineyards). But these prosperous buildings do not display the extravagant charm of the châteaux of Bordeaux, nor the inimitable cachet of the hamlets of Burgundy. The same holds true for the countryside and the surrounding vineyards.

The Champagne wine-growing region, which extends over five different *départements* but has its heart and soul in the Marne, is a hard, cold land. Everywhere it is scarred by traces of its tragic past as a battlefield for European conflicts down the centuries; it must atone for the painful martyrdom of the landscape through its intractable soil which only grudgingly yields its natural generosity.

The secret of champagne's excellence is revealed modestly, without ostentation. It rises to the surface of the soil in winter, in the immaculate whiteness of a chalky slope overlooking the Marne River, or describing an arc across the famous vineyards of the aptly named Côte des Blancs (though the "white" derives not from the soil, but from the sole variety of grape grown here, the white Chardonnay). But if chalk has endowed this soil with a character as precious as it is unique, the most original feature of the region certainly lies in the extraordinary talent that the inhabitants have displayed in creating an incomparable wine.

In such a cool, northerly climate, it is difficult to harvest grapes that will produce an opulent, strongly alcoholic wine. As early as the Middle Ages, wines from the Champagne region were described as light and lively, two adjectives that have not always been intended as praise. But champagne's social and commercial status changed abruptly when, in the early eighteenth century, it became a sparkling wine. According to legend, it was Dom Pérignon, a monk who ran the cellar at the abbey of Hautvillers, a wine-growing village overlooking Épernay and the Marne Valley, who discovered the quasi-divine technique that was to

Contrary to common belief, champagne is a wine that ages perfectly. It has already aged prior to reaching the market since it has remained in a cellar for three years, sometimes even as long as six or eight years for prestige champagnes or vintage years. But good quality champagnes, both white and pink, can also acquire a more mature style perhaps less of an aperitif but perfectly suited to the accompaniment of white meat or fish in sauce, through being laid down for several years—or even decades. Some firms, notably Bollinger, mature their best vintages in the cellar for years, disgorging it just prior to marketing in order to endow the wine with maximum freshness. *Above*: Charbant pink champagne. *Right*: Charbant white champagne

transform the modest wine of an inhospitable region into a sparkling nectar that would meet universal acclaim. In fact, Dom Pérignon simply composed a method on the various oenological experiments being carried out at the time, thereby setting down the veritable law of modern champagne.

One of the main driving forces behind champagne—and numerous other sparkling wines—lies in a second fermentation which takes place not in the vat, just after picking, but in the bottle. There is nothing exceptional about this phenomenon, which even today may occur against the winemaker's wishes. Fermentation is triggered by the simultaneous presence of yeasts and sugar. In the days when these processes were shrouded in the mystery of creation, it was common for "finished wine" to retain a certain proportion of sugar, the result of cold spells in the autumn which froze the action of the yeast before it had completed its work. Anaesthetized by the cold weather, the yeast cells went to sleep, leaving part of the grapes' natural sugar unfermented. Once the wine returned to warmer conditions, the yeasts rapidly went back to work, and the fermentation process began again.

As we have seen, the fermentation of sugar into alcohol gives off carbon dioxide. In an open vat, the gas immediately disperses into the air. But in a cask or bottle (which became the conventional container for wine only in the late seventeenth century), the gas created pressure and added bubbles to the liquid. All sailors who transported casks of wine in the hulls of their ships were familiar with the phe-

nomenon—it was not uncommon for one or several casks to explode or shatter under the pressure of the gas. The genius of Dom Pérignon and his contemporaries was to harness this disavantage and transform it into an incomparable advantage.

When glass bottles became the most sought-after containers for fine wines, this second fermentation systematically took place in the bottle. Originally, it consisted of a straightforward bottle fermentation brought about by the presence of a high degree of residual sugar. The heat of ships' hulls stimulated the yeasts which triggered fermentation once again. The bottles shattered under this unexpected pressure.

Even today, champagne producers anticipate a margin of breakage of roughly one percent. In any event, the preferred route of escape for the carbon dioxide is obviously the neck of the bottle. For many years corks were lashed to the bottle with a string, which was later replaced by metallic wire, to give the now-traditional cap known in French as a *muselet*. For bottles destined to age in the cellar after this second fermentation however, more rustic and less costly systems are used, beginning with simple aluminum caps like the ones used on beer bottles.

Such caps are used because the bottles will have to be opened one last time before being sold to customers, in order to remove the lees, or sediment. This urgent necessity lay at the origins of what was long a veritable art in the region, namely "riddling" (or turning) the bottles, followed by "disgorging" (or removal of sediment). Since the sediment is extremely fine and volatile, it is no easy matter to

Above: Until the nineteenth century, champagne corks were held in place by a carefully knotted length of hemp. Then a system of metal wire and cap was invented, a device which popularized even further a drink which had already become a symbol of French wit and spirit, according to Voltaire in *Le Mondain*: "Of a wine from Aï, whose hurried froth / up from the bottle fast burst forth / sending the cork like a thunderbolt / it spoke, we laughed, as ceiling it smote. / This sparkling foam of fine, cool wine / Reflects us French, the way we shine. / The morrow, we know, brings other pleasures / Yet more dinners, and other treasures." *Left*: A bottle held upside down, prior to disgorging.

manœuvre it from the side of the bottle, where it collects when the bottles are on their sides, to the neck, where it can be removed. To this end, Champagne winemakers invented large racks honeycombed with holes into which the bottles could be inserted up to the shoulder, first in a horizontal position, then progressively more and more vertically. Over a thirty to ninety day period, an employee almost imperceptibly nudges the lees toward the cap by turning and shaking the bottle every day. These turning movements must be very subtle to avoid clouding the wine: the bottle is rotated from the base, an eighth of a turn in one direction one day, an eighth in the other direction the next day. This repetitive task nevertheless requires a serious knack—a good turner can manipulate 60,000 bottles per day! At the conclusion of this slow process, the sediment is ready to be removed.

Champagne makers in the past (and a few small and skilled producers today) followed the practice of removing the sediment "on the fly", by removing the cap with a sharp knock that carried the lees with it, then immediately recapping the bottle with a minimum loss of pressure. Practical and shrewd, champagne makers take advantage of this fleeting moment to add a final touch to the taste of the wine. Now is the time to "dose" the champagne. There are several types of champagne: some (known, illogically enough, as *sec* or "dry") are sweet, designed to accompany desserts; others, more common and described as *brut* or *extra-brut*, are livelier and contain very little sugar. These varying degrees of sweetness are determined at this point, by the relative proportions of sugar syrup and pure champagne poured into the bottle to top it up.

All these meticulous and highly specific operations used to be carried out by hand. The dexterity of a riddler or the skill of a disgorger could significantly contribute to a producer's reputation. These days, with very few exceptions, riddling, disgorging and dosing are done by machines. The human touch nevertheless remains crucial for the truly qualitative decisions of length of aging on lees and selected dosage. Few wines require a development as complex as champagne, and few wines so fully display the human inventiveness that can transform a handicap into an advantage, or a hard and rigid landscape into a universal symbol of gaiety and elegance.

THE SECRET IS IN THE CASK

No wine—champagne or sparkling wine, white wine or red—is born in a day. On the contrary, they age and mature for varying lenghts of time from the moment they are pressed at harvest until they are finally put in the bottle. For the finest reds, this maturation process might last two years or longer. Yet only a few days after harvest, the must from the grapes has already become wine that can be drunk as it is; a few weeks later, the red wine is separated from the "cap" composed of the grape skins, and is transferred to a vat where it may quietly continue its existence free from any contact with the outside world. From this point onward, it is permissible to consider bottling and drinking the wine. This is precisely the process used for

Above and *right*: Traditional riddling racks for champagne at the Roederer firm in Reims, where the sediment caused by the formation of bubbles is steadily tilted toward the neck. In the process of *remuage*, a turner rotates each bottle every day by a few inches, all the while increasing the angle of the bottle a little. Even though professional riddlers are able to tend several thousand bottles per day, this slow, costly process is increasingly being entrusted to automatic machines, in the form of gyro-palettes programmed to conduct the operation on several dozen bottles at the same time. When it comes to larger bottles, however, like the magnums shown here, riddling is still done by hand.

wines drunk young (known as new wines, or *primeurs*), of which the most famous is Beaujolais Nouveau: harvested in September, made into wine within the month, put into vats immediately and bottled by early November, in order to be shipped around the globe on the third Thursday in November at midnight sharp! Wines made in this manner retain all the charm of the fresh fruit.

Oenologists specializing in the production of these wines have moreover invented a special technique of vinification, in which the grapes are not crushed, in order to reduce as far as possible the presence of astringent tannins that are incompatible with the light and fruity qualities expected of these wines.

For other vintages, however, autumn signals the start of a period of almost monastic retreat. Leaving the world of the production cellar, the young wine from great vineyards abandons definitively the rows of stainless steel vats, pumps and pipes, the computers monitoring the ambient temperature, the clinical hygiene and bright lighting, the bustle of employees and cellar masters checking, controlling and shaping its future. It moves to another cellar with a completely different ambiance: now it enters the heart of the cult of winemaking, a space that feels like a chapel in some timeless abbey, where light is rare and silence all-encompassing.

Such cellars in Pauillac (France), Sonoma (California) or Mendoza (Argentina), take on the air of a cathedral of profound and solemn luxury. In Vosne-Romanée (Burgundy), Jerez (Spain) or Barolo (Italy), meanwhile, they assume the sombre appearance of a medieval

monastery, their Romanesque vaults clothed with centuries-old moss. Instead of prayer stools, the servants of this pagan cult have set up oak casks. Strictly aligned one behind another, in serried rows of golden brown, these barrels will receive the wine for its long retreat devoted to contemplation and an intense inner life.

Wine cannot be aged in any old wood. From time immemorial, majestic oaks have played their part in the creation of great wines. For many years, oak and stone were the only materials used by winemakers, some of whom have now revived the taste for the traditional large cylindrical vats without covers. During the course of the twentieth century, cement and later stainless steel vats delivered a seemingly mortal blow to oak's supremacy. Both these new materials offered numerous advantages to seduce wine producers: they are more economical (especially cement), permit the construction of much larger vats (eliminating the need to invest in new buildings for additional surface area), are completely leak-proof and easy to clean (therefore less likely to transmit any outside contamination to the wine), and their lifespan is much greater than that of wood. For all these reasons, cement and steel became the materials for vats used to make wines that were technically well produced but not particularly ambitious.

This is not the case for wines of a higher standard. In some vineyards barrel-aging has never really been abandoned; in others it has been resumed after being discontinued for a period (invariably for economic reasons, sometimes dressed up in vaguely oenological

"Wine is the child of sun and earth, but has to be delivered by a midwife. Like great works and great ideas, it does not spring from the press ready to be gulped down by a greedy, inattentive belly. It demands a combination of craft, patience, time, and attention. It requires a long journey through the dark in order to yield a masterpiece of flavors that dazzles the mind as much as the tongue." In his *Éloge du Vin,* Paul Claudel paid due tribute to the time and patience of maturation, crucial to the development of a great wine. *Above*: The bunghole of a cask, stopped with a cork covered with oiled hempen cloth (others exist in silicon or glass). *Right*: Racking wine from a barrel in the Domecq sherry *bodega* in Jerez.

terms). In all recently established vineyards, ambitious producers have without hesitation opted to use casks. This passion is fuelled by one key factor: wood does not merely provide an inert lining in which the wine is contained for a time, but instead plays an active part in the crucial process known as *élevage*, or maturation.

Since he succeeded his father in the small family concern he had built up at Ampuis, an austere village on the banks of the Rhône, Marcel Guigal has brought his Côte Rôtie wines to the attention of connoisseurs the world over, who snap up his finest vintages at astronomical prices. This red wine from the Côtes du Rhône area is famous for the almost wild power of its body and the entrancing vigor of its bewitching flavor. Guigal, cap

constantly on head, tames this tremendous bull of a wine by means of a long maturation—over three years!—in new oak. Tirelessly, he threads his way through the warren of underground rooms and corridors that make up his cellar, monitoring the development of his treasures, plunging his pipette into the bunghole of a barrel to taste the wine and follow the maturation process on an almost daily basis.

In the rich vocabulary of winemaking, no term is more evocative than that of *élevage*, with its overtones of a young man's rite of passage into the adult world. With Guigal, the analogy becomes almost paternal, as he watches over each wine, allowing it to rest after the tumultuous event that accompanied its birth, but also giving this thoroughbred the

Above: The cask-lined wine cellar of the Tuscan abbey of Badia Passignano. Wine cellars are often compared with cathedrals, and the two certainly share characteristics of silence and a cool, constant temperature. Wine is highly sensitive to the surrounding temperature. A cold atmosphere, as often occurs in winter, will halt all biochemical activity, for example the auxiliary fermentation process known as malolactic fermentation, which occurs in the cask, but which will begin again once the temperature rises. More serious are the effects of great heat, which threaten to accelerate the aging of the wine and increase evaporation in each barrel (thereby increasing the risk of oxidation).

opportunity to draw new strength, rich body and elegant texture from this time of retreat. Finally, he decks it out in fresh finery so that it may serenely complete its aging in the bottle, in the depths of a cellar belonging to one of its worshippers.

Some thirty years ago, when Guigal decided to renew his stock of barrels on a regular basis, he was taken for a madman in a region where winemakers traditionally put their wine in ancient casks handed down by previous generations. For the precise nature of the interaction between wood and wine was little understood for many years. Some of the benefits of wood are related to its very nature as a material, others to the modest size of the casks it is used to make. Wood acts as a filter, allowing infinitesimal quantities of oxygen to com-

bine with the liquid. Because of its ability to oxidize all food and drink and rapidly make them unfit for consumption, air is undoubtedly one of wine's greatest enemies: you need only leave a half-empty bottle of wine open for a day or two to observe its damaging effects. But, just as Mithridates immunized himself against poisons by rubbing tiny amounts of venom into his wounds, wine manages to ward off the dangers of oxidation through this beneficial and extremely limited contact with the oxygen surrounding the oak. Its is an exchange which has its perils, nevertheless, since the slow but inevitable evaporation of a tiny quantity of liquid in the barrel considerably increases the risks of oxidation. It is to avoid this problem that, at Ampuis and elsewhere, winemakers regularly replace the

A few rare estates, such as Bel Air in Saint-Émilion, are able to place their casks in caverns naturally hollowed out of the limestone. With their constant temperature and humidity, these caves present outstanding conditions for aging great wines. Some estates in Champagne also benefit from these conditions, such as the Ruinart firm which matures its wines in chalk pits dug as quarries during the Gallo-Roman period. Sadly, most wine cellars have to be specially built for the purpose. This necessity has nevertheless provided prestigious estates with the opportunity to commission a famous architect to design one of these primordial spaces. The following pages show the impressive wine cellar designed by Ricardo Bofill for Château Lafite.

lost wine by topping up the casks to the level of the bunghole.

Conversely, wine living with its sediment in such a small container—228 liters in a traditional barrel—must be allowed to "breathe" from time to time in order to prevent a phenomenon of reduction that lends the wine an unpleasant taste and aroma reminiscent, not surprisingly, of an overpowering mustiness. This is the reason why Guigal regularly "racks" his wine, decanting it from one cask to another and thereby separating the liquid from the deposit that has settled at the bottom. Where less careful winemakers might take weeks to even notice a problem, Guigal's heightened palate alerts him immediately to the need for such an operation. Occasionally, maturation requires a truly artistic sensitivity.

Finally, wood gives part of itself to the wine. Like all woody vegetable matter, it possesses tannins, which seep into the wine and lend it added structure. The lees, meanwhile —which can be wine's worst enemy or its finest ally—will enrich the hard, thin tannins of the wood to add welcome suppleness and lushness.

Naturally there exist numerous different winemaking techniques, more or less well adapted to local traditions, to the style of given wines and to the characteristics of the grapes used. In some regions, the wine is transferred almost immediately from the fermenting vat, where it is in contact with the crushed grapes, to the barrels. In others, it is placed initially in another vat of stainless steel or cement, where it is left to get on by itself with a new and complementary modification of its constitutional balance, in a process known as malolactic fermentation. During this fermentation—so discreet that its secrets were deciphered by Pasteur just a century ago and has only been understood by most winemakers for only a few decades—certain acids are modified in such a way as to lend the wine added roundness and harmony. The lees also

play a specific role by transforming some of the wine's substances into others with different sensory characteristics, altering both its taste and its texture.

This aspect is crucial to white wines. In the enormous wineries of South Australia, such as Penfold's and Petaluma, serried rows of casks stand awaiting for wine pressed from Chardonnay grapes which, opulent and flattering, will marry its aromas of fresh butter and nuts with hints of vanilla and caramel from the lightly charred oak of the staves. The rapid charring of the inner lining of the oak is designed to produce a double effect. First it gives a curved shape to the staves, and secondly, thanks to the caramelization of certain substances in the wood, il provides the wine with additional bouquet. The more the wood is

Debate has raged for over a century concerning the use of oak casks to age wine for a few months or several years. Cement, followed by stainless steel, was for decades thought to be an improvement on less hygienic wood. Then winemakers began realize that a clean, healthy cask allowed the wine the valuable opportunity to breathe a little, which was not possible inside perfectly airtight containers. The debate then shifted to old oak versus new. New wood contributes additional tannin and aromas to the wine, which is an advantage for wines sufficiently concentrated to assimilate them, but otherwise amounts to doctoring.

Left: Old oak casks for aging Solera Banyuls, a fortified wine made here by Cellier des Templiers. *Above*: A delivery of new casks at Casa Lapostolle in Chile.

heated, the more intense the roasted, caramelized flavor.

Australian oenologists handle the Burgundian Chardonnay grape in much the same way as winemakers in Burgundy, but on a giant, systematic scale. The wine is "beaten" every day: using a thin stem placed in the cask through the bunghole, the lees are stirred to make the dead yeast mix with the liquid. The action of the yeasts, even when dead, is crucial, the deposit of fine gray powder literally nourishing the wine and offering it the extraordinary opportunity to become more attractive, smoother and lusher, acquiring a rich, complex bouquet.

Sometimes the advantages of oak are perceived solely in terms of an added aroma, to the extent that there now exist techniques for imparting a totally natural woody taste through the addition of oak-chip liqueurs. This eliminates the necessity of buying and maintaining a stock of barrels. Vintages such as these, produced more or less everywhere in the world, are nothing more than a con; wine may sometimes be a mirror of its time, even when the latter values appearances above simply being.

After two or three seasons, meanwhile, casks used to age wine year after year will lose all their properties apart from that of filtering oxygen. Great estates the world over therefore replace a good percentage of their barrels every year, in order to provide their wines with containers worthy of their ambitions. All these estates are extremely demanding when it comes not only to the supplier, but also to the origins of the oak used, and the way the staves are heated when making the barrel.

Like grapevines, oak trees prosper in certain soils and climate. Slovenian forests, dark and majestic, were once the most highly reputed. Oak was also imported from Hungary at great expense. When war and the advent of communism almost completely dried up that source, cask-makers (most of whom were

French) turned to the forests of France, and trees in the Allier, Nivernais and Vosges regions soon established their pedigree. In addition to the quality of the planting and management of different forests, there also exist enormous discrepancies in the grain depending on its origins: one wood will be coarse and grainy to the touch, while another will display altogether remarkable finesse and density of texture.

The most highly reputed oak is indisputably from the Tronçais forest in the Allier, region of central France. If all the winemakers the world over who claim that their casks come from this miraculous forest were to be believed, the Tronçais would have been stripped of its trees long ago! Oak requires a professional approach; the cycle of renewal for an oak forest takes 160 years, and coopers use only the heart of the trunk, called the *merrain*, to make their staves. Unlike the traditional way of cutting wood for furniture, stave wood is not sawed but rather split lengthwise, so that the strata of the wood are followed perfectly, without beeing broken. After being dried in a kiln or in the open air, which is better but takes several years, the planks are made into staves. In order to fit them together and hoop them, the cooper slightly curves the staves by heating the inner side with a naked flame. It quickly became clear that different intensities of firing would impart different flavors to the wine in the barrels—the stronger the firing, the more intimately the roasted aromas of vanilla and caramel will be wedded to the wine's own flavors.

Over the past thirty years, oak and barrels have thus embarked on a new relationship with wine, incalculably more closely studied and managed than it had ever been in the preceding twenty centuries—to the point where certain bottles now flaunt an overpowering oakiness that makes it difficult to discern the wine beneath. But used well and

Numbering the staves—split, rather than sawn, from the trunk of an oak, in order to respect the natural veins and ridges and also increase watertightness—prior to final assembly with metal hoops at Séguin-Moreau in Cognac, one of the largest cask-making firms in the world. Until quite recently, cognac companies were the main customers for new oak, which explains why so many coopers are to be found in the Charentes region. But the world-wide vogue for aging red and white wines in new casks has given these firms new impetus. Their plans for future development now hinge on finding new sources of oak, notably in Russian or American forests.

wisely, oak brings out the best in a great wine. What was once the soil and climate, on which vines flourish, and then a grape harvest transformed by an accumulation of techniques into an alcoholic drink, finally attains its culmination: soil, vineyard, and grapes have together given birth to a vintage wine.

FROM BARK TO CORK,
FROM GLASS TO BOTTLE

Only one task now remains: to get this wild youth (or elegant aristocrat) into the bottle. The operation is not a simple one, and depends primarily—and somewhat unromantically—on the nature of the materials used. This issue provides specialists with a fresh opportunity for cutthroat disputes over whether it is best not to filter the wine prior to bottling in order

to retain all its qualities intact or on the contrary to filter it to obtain a pure, limpid appearance, above all to enable it to withstand on the ill-treatment it will inevitably encounter when in the bottle.

Whatever the decision, the wine ultimately ends up in a standard bottle of 750 milliliters (3/4 of a liter), or sometimes in a magnum (1.5 liters), a jeroboam (3 liters), or an even more formidable container such as a balthazar (12 liters) or nebuchadnezzar (15 liters). But at the very last moment more magic occurs, in the startling encounter between the fruit of the vine and the product of a tree of equally ancient lineage and powerful symbolism: the cork-oak. It is a remarkable, age-old story, well worth the telling.

The only tool used by Victor, a sturdy peasant farmer in the Algarve region of Portugal, is an old but elegant hatchet. He first carefully

Like all planks, staves are initially flat, and have to be bent to form the curving lines of a barrel. Lighting a fire inside the cask (*above*, in the François cooperage at Saint-Romain in Burgundy), lends the wood a natural curve. This heat treatment moreover gives rise to charred flavors inside the barrel that will harmonize with the wine. *Right*: A cellar on the Tuscan estate of Castello di Ama. Note that the barrels are positioned with the bunghole on top, and that each hole is simply covered by a heavy glass cylinder. Staff can thus monitor the progress of the malolactic fermentation which produces carbon dioxide. When the wine has settled down, the barrel will be sealed more hermetically with a stopper of wood or silicon and turned on its side to keep the stopper moist.

marks out the upper and lower edges of the area to be attacked—bark is stripped only from around the main trunk and sometimes, on large old trees, from the two or three main branches growing from it. After having made a circular cut top and bottom, without touching the wood with the blade, Victor begins to split the cork lengthwise. This is a technique which clearly demands perfect mastery: ordinary mortals would soon either strike too deep (wounding the tree and preventing any cork from growing again around the wound) or miss the line of the split that half-opens with each blow of the hatchet, following the most obvious fissures.

Moreover, Victor is able to select at a glance a tree whose bark seems ready to come off without too much trouble, before setting to work on the north side of the tree (which theoretically offers the most resistance). Halfway down the first split, the layer of cork can already be seen coming away from the trunk. Victor finishes the job by pulling the two sides apart. Gently using the handle of his hatchet as a lever, he then removes the bark from the tree completely.

In this poor southern region of Portugal, it is not possible to make a full-time living from cork-stripping. It is an activity traditionally carried out by farmers alongside their other agricultural work. But the rural exodus taking place here, too, means that the skill is slowly being lost. Victor is nevertheless proud of this delicate work which he has practised in late summer every year since his early youth, climbing nimbly up the long-suffering trees, identifying with a swift glance the fissures that make splitting easy, and sinking his hatchet

with just the right degree of force, neither too gently nor too brutally. He is proud of this craft, anchored in local tradition, which has given him, at over seventy years of age, the thin and wiry appearance of a young man.

Victor is just one link in the long chain leading from the cork on the tree to the cork in the bottle, but he symbolizes perfectly the profound love of the craft that unites all the professionals in this little-known industry.

Although bottles began to appear in apothecary shops after the Renaissance, they were not used for wine until the reign of Louis XIV in the seventeenth century. And even then they were used only for the few minutes that separated the cask from the table. Bottles at this time were hand-blown, and so their necks were never exactly the same size. To close them, cone-shaped cork stoppers that could adapt to every diameter were sometimes used, but the most fashionable stoppers were made of oil-soaked hemp. Whether of hemp or cork, these stoppers were rarely hermetic. So it was common practice to pour a thin layer of oil over the wine to prevent oxidation—a practice commemorated in the present-day habit of pouring the first drops from the bottle into one's own glass before serving guests.

"Corks" made of cork really came into their own during the early eighteenth century. Advances in glass-making led to the production, initially in England, of bottles in strong, dark glass with a reliably calibrated neck, making it possible to insert methodically the first cylindrical corks which were then carefully lashed to the bottle.

Above and *right*: A bark-stripper from São Bartolomeo, wielding a hatchet similar to the one used by his father and grandfather, performs almost ritual gestures when working the trunk of a cork-oak. Forests of cork-oak are vast and well maintained in this part of southern Portugal. There is never a lack of raw material, even though the bark of the oak takes nine years to grow back to the thickness seen here. Most stands of cork-oak belong to private estates, but the specific task of bark-stripping has never been a full-time job—it provides extra work in a region where the agricultural life is hard and impoverished.

At this time, cork-makers cut individual corks one by one, using a slender knife: skilled worker could turn out up to 2,000 corks per day, a figure which prompts speculation as to just how watertight they were.

Bottles gradually began to appear on the table (prior to that, goblets of wine or water had been brought to the table by cupbearers, who took them away again as soon as the guest had drunk), and the industry was steadily rationalized. Shapes became taller, stretching from the flask or pear-shaped bottle still used for certain Armagnacs to the shape now used in Burgundy, and the size and appearance of necks became standardized. By 1829, half the annual revenues of French glass-makers came from the production of bottles, estimated at a figure of 115 million in 1868, to double before the nineteenth century was out.

The cork industry also sought to rationalize itself, although with less rigor. In the first half of the twentieth century many conical corks were still being used for ordinary table wines, and it was the only the spread of completely automated bottling and corking machinery that made an accurate calibration of corks imperative. This was already the case for the great vintages of the nineteenth century, and the quality of corks in those days was quite as good as in those of today.

Unlike other industries, cork production has never experienced problems with supplies of raw materials, since cork-oaks are one of the longest-establishes trees of the Mediterranean basin. Growing naturally on siliceous soils—sandy, schisty, or old granitic—they are able to adapt to hot, dry climates yet appreciate maritime influences, and are happy either in mountains or on flat land. In areas where few plants thrive, cork-oaks enjoy an exceptionally long and vigorous life (cork can still be harvested from trees 150 years old). On the other hand, apart from its bark the tree has little to offer—its wood is useless for carpentry and its acorns are prized only by the wild boars and black pigs of Estremadura in Spain.

In the first half of the twentieth century, cork was worked in numerous forests around the Mediterranean, in southern France, Corsica, Catalonia, Estremadura, Sardinia, Sicily, the coastal regions of Algeria and Tunisia, and the southern coasts of the Atlantic (western Morocco and southern Portugal). Modest agricultural returns and a scarcity of labor slowly choked production on certain European plantations, such as those in the Var region of France. Decolonization, meanwhile, put an end to the exploitation of North African forests.

Nowadays, most cork comes from southern Portugal and Spain or, less frequently, from Corsica and Sardinia. Cultivating cork-oaks is hardly the surest way of making a fortune. Once planted, the trees only become productive after thirty years. From that point on, they may be stripped of cork every nine (or sometimes ten) years, the interval necessary for a sufficiently thick bark to grow back.

Once the cork has been harvested, the long journey that will ultimately end in the neck of a bottle can begin. The stripped cork is first stacked by the tree owner or a local trader. The sheets, in the form of a semi-circle repre-

Dried in the open air after having been dipped in boiling water to flatten it, the cork hardens and sometimes even cracks, but never loses its elasticity. These sheets of cork, more than a foot long and as broad as the circumference of the tree trunk, are stacked outdoors in the courtyard of the village wholesaler, awaiting the arrival of a broker from a cork manufacturer in northern Portugal. The broker's trained eye will examine the stacks, eliminating those that contain too many sheets which are cracked, stained by green sap, or simply too thin. Rejected bark will be pulped to make panels of agglomerated cork.

senting half of the diameter of the trunk or branch from which they were stripped, spend at least one winter outdoors. Formerly they would stand for an entire year, but the demands of modern industry have reduced this aging period. As with the oak destined to be made into casks, exposure to the elements—a succession of rain and dry weather, hot temperatures and cold—eliminates a certain number of mineral salts present in the cork.

The cork is then flattened in boiling water, which cleanses it of certain impurities and swells it. Then it is left to rest in the open air for three to four weeks, during which time it acquires its elasticity. It is then carefully sorted, each sheet being scrupulously examined for defects—dampness, spots of sap (which inhibit elasticity), crevices and holes, tunnels made by ants or worms, and other faults which render it unsuitable for making natural cork stoppers. Sheets that pass the test are then graded into six levels of quality.

Cut in strips a few centimeters thick and calibrated to the desired length of the finished cork (from 38 to 54 millimeters, 44 millimeters being the most common), the cork is then introduced into a cork-cutting machine which cuts out the cylinders. The operator must have a good eye in order to cut the cylinder as near as possible to the crusty outer surface without actually touching it, watching out all the while for fingers that come perilously close to the blades of the machine. Mechanized though it may be, the cork industry remains resolutely unautomated, with factories that give off an old-fashioned air.

Once trimmed and ground, the cork reaches the desired size. Does that mean it is finished? Of course not: it must now be washed and disinfected i order to meet current standards governing products that come to contact with food.

By this stage, the corks have often left their country of origin and arrived at the wholesaler, where they will be checked again, sorted into various categories according to qualities, and possibly rejected. Very often this sorting operation is still done manually, by female employees who with a skilled eye pick out defective corks as they pass between their fingers on a conveyor belt. There also exist computerized systems which analyze and photograph the corks' external appearance, automatically eliminating corks that do not meet the predefined standards.

Now the corks need only to be dressed for their final handler, the wine-producer. According to the winemaker's wishes, they may be stamped with the crest of the estate and the year of the wine, using either an ink-printing technique or heat-engraving. Then they are dusted, and the surface treated with paraffin wax or silicon to make their future removal from the bottle easier. After one last sorting operation, they are finally ready for shipping.

Corks have been known to cause problems. The notorious "corked" taste, the subject of so many tight-lipped and hasty exchanges with contrite or skeptical wine-stewards, remains a common cause of embarrassment. Research into this problem has demonstrated that there may be a variety of causes behind an allegedly "corked" wine. A yellow stain in the cork, or

The manufacture of corks has been greatly modernized, and today's big firms are at the cutting edge of computer-aided monitoring and quality-control techniques at all stages of production. Yet some smaller companies still use very basic equipment, which occasionally poses serious risks for workers. This tube-drill, for instance (*above*) can cut a finger as easily as a cork, and is not recommended for beginners. Meanwhile, at the marketing end of the production chain, some cork wholesalers simply buy up batches of corks at a low price and without any quality control, selling them to wine-producers who believe they are getting a good deal. Although such corks do not present a risk to health, they are responsible for most of the bottles that taste "corked."

fresh sap (a greenish stain), defective micro-biological conditions, poorly controlled washing and disinfection techniques, or incompetent surface treatment (of paraffin or silicon) are the causes that may be directly attributed to the cork. On the other hand, if a bottle is poorly rinsed prior to being filled with wine, if the products used for cleaning the filters, pipes or spigots employed in the fermentation process have not been thoroughly eliminated, if the corks have been stored in dirty premises or, on the contrary, are impregnated with the smell of certain household cleaners, weed-killers and insecticides used in the vineyard or wood treatments, then the wine may well have an unpleasant taste that is mistakenly described as "corked." Finally, maturation in a cask that is too old and of poor quality can give the wine a harsh, corky taste that drinkers too often attribute to the cork itself. In short, glass in hand, the connoisseur rapidly comes to appreciate the importance of this final link in a wine's great chain of creation.

"Now, I have two types of wine, you understand: one has a red seal—it is an 1846 Cos d'Estournel, a most beneficial wine which I save for myself; the other, with a green seal, is a Mâcon which is generous, but suits me less well. So you will serve the green seal to my friends, while you give the red seal to me, and me alone—without anyone noticing, of course." Eugène Labiche, *Moi*, Act III. The private cellars of great estates in Médoc (*right*, Château Lafite) are still stacked high with such legendary vintages, although in this case a few fortunate and extremely select guests are sometimes entitled to drink them. *Above*: A cork from another legendary wine, Château Margaux. *Following pages*: The initials of the Roederer champagne firm (*left*) and a detail from the door to the Burmester cellars in Vila Nova de Gaia (*right*).

A
Tale
of
Trade

At the conclusion of this saga in which the gifts of nature are so closely interwoven with those of men and women, wine is usually incarcerated in a small, 750-milliliter bottle. Yet far from remaining inert, it now begins a second life in this glass shell, though a much less tumultuous one than its first existence in vat or barrel. Its highly expressive, youthful aromas of fresh fruit and flowers will steadily evolve and develop into a complex and subtle bouquet, its components will blend and mature with time, and its color will take on golden highlights or a fine moiré sheen.

Countless wines only experience a short and simple version of this second life, while other, much rarer ones, will enjoy a long and dazzling career. These are members of the elite of great wines produced at the finest estates, from Château Margaux in Bordeaux to Robert Mondavi's reserves in California, from Schloss Johannisberg in Germany to the Gaja estate in Italy. But in order to gain entrance to this exclusive club, wines must still be able to meet their public. And of all the stages in the making of a wine, marketing is by no means the least compelling. On the contrary, it is a sphere in which people have demonstrated an inventiveness and business acumen ranging from the completely ludicrous to the utterly inspired.

THE PERSONALITY OF A WINE

With its log-cabin construction, small-pared windows and its finely carved doors, the Beringer homestead seems straight out of Snow White and the Seven Dwarfs. And if the surrounding countryside bears little resemblance to romantic Teutonic forests, this is because we are now less than 600 miles from Hollywood, in the cool vine-planted valleys of northern California. Inside the winery, a squad of smiling young women offers the firm's products to a clientele equally composed of fun-loving, noisy tourists and glass-sniffing wine connoisseurs (who plunge their eyes into a guide to know what they should think of the nectar they are tasting).

The winery's large, welcoming shopping center contains a wide range of products proudly displayed on blond-wood shelves and in subtly decorated display cases—bottles of wine, naturally, but also clothing, sweatshirts, scarves and baseball caps, countless gadgets, books, miniature reproductions of the winery, and a broad selecion of semi-homemade preserves packaged in pretty glass jars. The vineyard's various varieties of grape have been adapted—literally—to every taste, from Cabernet Sauvignon or Merlot jam to

All wines are welcome at the dinner table, from this year's wine to the venerable vintage, from the famous to the new discovery, from red to white, from the ancient, award-winning estate to the ambitious newcomer. The two labels on these pages embody perfectly the versatility of wine's evocative powers. *Left*: The star wine from Cain Winery in Saint Helena is dubbed "Five" because it is blended from five varieties, all proudly indicated on the label, down to the exact percentage of each. *Above*: Separated from California by a continent, an ocean, and nearly 1,000 years of history is Schloss Johannisberg, a legendary estate and wine from the Rheingau region of Germany, founded by Benedictine monks from Mainz, and pioneer in the harvesting of Riesling grapes with "noble rot." Napoleon presented it as a gift to his general, Kellerman, until the Congress of Vienna awarded it to Metternich (whose family still owns it). What possible connection can there be between these two wines, if not the pleasure they bring to wine-lovers?

Syrah-flavored spaghetti sauce and Gewürz-traminer cream. The one common feature of this extraordinary range of products, aimed at every level and taste, is to be found printed on all the fabrics and every jam jar and bottle label: the winery's logo, designed with extreme care and meticulous research that its hand-lettered name seems straight out of the heroic days of the Far West. But the tiny letter R set in a circle betrays modern-day concerns, breaking the hand-written charm—for the winery was only founded in the mid 1970s. In a land where marketing is king, such commercial enthusiasm is hardly surprising. Nor is it incongruous when applied to wine. On the contrary, a concern to distinguish oneself from one's neighbor and competitor has always been part of the intense ferment of activity surrounding the wine-producing business.

Even though the transformation of the names of châteaux and estates into veritable brand names dates only from a relatively recent past—the end of the seventeenth century for certain Bordeaux vintages, the eighteenth for the signature of the great British, Dutch and German wine merchants—wine dealers have always sought ways of calling attention to their product. The name of the vineyard of origin was long the sole, if highly evocative, means of attractive interest. A hundred years before the birth of Christ, Roman patricians sang the praises of vintages from Falernum, a small village on the road between Rome and Naples. Falernum produced several types of wine, some of them powerful and highly alcoholic, others sweet and smooth with aromas of honey. With a few other villages scattered throughout Roman Italy, it shared the privilege of hearing its name cited as a symbol of excellence by every hedonist in the empire.

In the Middle Ages, city—and town—dwellers were essentially supplied with wines from the surrounding vineyards. Local farm produce, including wine, entered the city gates freely, whereas goods from further abroad were heavily taxed for the right to be put on sale in the town's markets and stalls. In the cities of northern Europe it hardly mattered if unsuitable soil and harsh climate limited the quality of local wines, as the public at large knew only these and were obliged to get used to them. Only the most powerful members of the nobility had the opportunity to discover other vintages, on journeys to make war or to contract dynastic marriages. Carried away by the memory of such events as much as by the pleasure of tasting an exotic wine, they would enthuse about it and officially vaunt its merits. Even today, it is not unusual to see a sign at the entrance to a village or in a tourist brochure boasting that centuries ago some tiny European vineyard produced the "favorite wine" of this or that king. Some monarchs seem to have been blithely prodigal in their praises, moreover: Henry IV, king of France and Navarre, left countless French villages claiming to be the home of his favorite wine, from Jurançon (with which his lips were moistened on the day of his baptism, as garlic was held under the infant nose) to Tavel (whose opulent rosé wine he adored).

The unique reputation of Bordeaux's vineyards was built not only by dynasties of British, German and Dutch traders, but also by the region's great families, some of whom gave rise to remarkable sagas. Château Pichon-Comtesse de Lalande, for example, is one of the very rare estates to have been run largely by women throughout its history. Marie-Laure Virginie de Pichon Longueville, Comtesse de Lalande (*above*), was the first of these female wine-growers. Born in 1798, she managed the estate from 1850 until her death in 1882, and saw her work rewarded with the prestigious classification of *deuxième cru* (just behind Lafite and Latour in Pauillac) during the official ranking in 1855 (which still holds today). The countess was succeeded by her great-niece Sophie de Lalande until 1916, and the estate is now run with remarkable dynamism by a third woman, May-Eliane de Lencquesaing.

THE ART OF COMMERCE

The British writer Hugh Johnson—perhaps the most famous of all writers on wine, along with Frenchman Raymond Dumay—likes to point out that no great wine can exist without a market, that is to say without merchants and consumers sufficiently demanding to buy such luxury products. Even if, as will be seen later, marketing savvy rather than savoir-faire might be called England's specific contribution to the elaboration of great wines, this is nevertheless a highly pertinent observation: since time immemorial, no wine has gained a reputation beyond the simple context of local consumption without the marketing skills of professional wine traders. And it was only logical that these merchants should come initially from lands or regions that produced no wine of their own.

Throughout the Middle Ages, a highly active wine trade thus developed in northern Europe, while the royal courts of France, Italy and Spain contented themselves with wines produced locally. By the Renaissance, people in England, Flanders, Holland, and the cities of the Hanseatic League, to the north of Germany, were drinking and enjoying hock from the Rhineland, clarets from Bordeaux and Gascony, and the wines of Spain and Portugal. All these wines were transported by maritime routes, and it is no coincidence that the reputation of the vineyards went hard with their ease of access by sea.

It was these countries of northern Europe, receptive to the new ideas of the Reformation, who devised and put into operation the main principles of economic free trade. In the seventeenth century, this commercial dynamism was driven primarily by the Dutch, and was applied initially to other beverages, as countless Flemish merchants who sailed the world's seas and set up trading posts in every port spread the vogue for "colonial infusions."

Above: A painting by Dutch artist Jan van Goyen (1596–1665), *Merchants on the Quay at Dordrecht* (Musée de Picardie, France). Holland and England were the two great wine trading nations. For centuries, their merchants conducted gruelling negotiations with often wily wine-growers who might well have resembled Balzac's brilliant description of Old Grandet, who here recounts a successful transaction: "'Wife,' he said without stammering, 'I got them all. Our wine is sold! The Dutch and the Belgians were leaving this morning. I took a stroll around the square, in front of their inn, with a fairly stupid air. What's-his-name, you know who, came up to me. The owners of all the fine vineyards are holding back their harvest; if they want to wait, I'll not prevent them. But our Belgian was getting desperate, I could see that. Deal concluded at two hundred francs per cask, half in cash. I was paid in gold. The bills are drawn up, here are six louis for you. In three months, the price of wine will drop.'"

The rules of serving at table were codified during the Middle Ages but underwent many changes during subsequent centuries, in faithfull reflection of changes in social customs. The seventeenth century—the century of absolute monarchy—imposed its desire for grandeur and pomp even in the way wines were served: it was poured in the pantry or at a nearby buffet, the glasses then being brought to the guests, who could thus continue their conversation without interruption. One such buffet is shown in this oil painting by Van der Lamen (1608–1651), entitled *Flirtatious Gathering* (Musée Angladon, Avignon).

At first this meant chocolate, brought from the Aztec empire, to seduce a public made up of an aristocracy and bourgeoisie in search of new tastes; in northern Europe, and especially England, people flocked to "chocolate houses" where they could sample this original drink in a good company. Almost immediately, however, a decoction of beans from a plant of Ethiopian origin, the coffee bush, also took northern Europe by storm. And by the end of the century, which set in place the foundations of modern trade, England opted definitively for its queen of beverages, discovered in the Far East by Portuguese explorers: tea. Having successfully launched these new drinks on the market, Dutch and British traders sought in parallel to develop their sales of alcoholic drinks. In these northern conutries, where every town and every neighborhood had its own brewer, beer remained the popular drink *par excellence*. The Flemish now launched an alcohol drink steeped with juniper berries, known as gin, which was such an overwhelming success in Britain that politicians and writers became exercised about the harm caused by alcoholism at every level of society. In the wake of gin, the same merchants offered wines briskly fortified with alcohol. For these wines, known as "brandy-wines" from the Dutch, *brandewijn*, or "burned wine", the quality of the original vintage mattered little, so that it could come from almost any vineyard. This taste for strong wines was to grow, to the detriment initially of traditional claret from Bordeaux—a light and supple wine at the time—and later encouraging public tastes in the direction of new drinks known as "black wines," the ancestors of today's port.

But the business of these traders—this time British—really took off once they began to sell not only anonymous wines from a given region of Europe, but also specific vintages corresponding to particular vineyards and wine-makers. Hitherto, a British wine merchant's stock list would have included only a few simple names: claret (covering all wine produced in Bordeaux), port, sack (later known as sherry), and so on. The nature of the trade was revolutionized when consumers started to demand one specifically identified vintage rather than another.

For the fun of it, let us give a precise date to this revolution: April 10, 1663. On that fine spring day, the London diarist Samuel Pepys went to his study immediately after taking diner at a tavern in the City of London, in order to write to a friend of a dazzlingly special wine: "Drank a sort of French wine, called Ho Bryan [Haut-Brion!], that hath a good and most particular taste that I ever met with." Quite apart from the fact that Pepys's description still holds good today, so inimitable do this wine's smoky character and bouquet remain, this modest comment is the first known written testimony of an attachment to a specific wine. It is more than likely, moreover, that Pepys's infatuation was widely shared by his fellow Britons, because Monsieur de Pontac, owner of Château Haut-Brion (and head magistrate of Bordeaux's *parlement*), opened a high-class restaurant in London, called Pontack's Head, which naturally gave pride of place to Haut-Brion and wines from his other domains.

From the early eighteenth century onwards, merchants promoted the glittering English reputation of vintages such as Haut-Brion, Lafite, Latour, and Margaux, casks of which would sell for three or four times more than other clarets. Sometimes, in a particularly good year, similar prices might be commanded by a wine from Hermitage in the Rhône Valley, a Burgundy from the Côte d'Or or, more

Founded in the seventeenth century and already famous by the eighteenth, the vineyards of Médoc adopted early on the form and infrastructure of vintage growths that we know today. Although many estates have been enlarged (or, conversely, subdivided) through inheritance or sale, very few vintages have totally disappeared (in contrast to the Graves region, which has suffered from the urban expansion of the outskirts of Bordeaux). Only one of the vintages ranked in 1855 no longer exists today, the obscure Château Dubignon. Equally rare—at least in the past century—is the creation of a totally new estate: one of the most ambitious examples is Château Clarke (*right*), founded in Listrac by Baron Edmond de Rothschild. A great collector of objects and furniture related to wine, the baron has transformed Château Clarke into an extraordinary homage to wine. Shown here is a specialized nineteenth-century English piece of furniture used by traders to store and file samples of their wines.

usually, a champagne in the new sweet and sparkling style.

Much less expensive were Spanish wines from Jerez (sherry), Malaga and Madeira, ports and Chiantis from Tuscany. Whites from the Rhine Valley, meanwhile, appealed to a clientele of aesthetes. It was at this time that a number of merchants set up London businesses which rapidly became masters in the art of tracking down the finest wines, such as like James Bennet, Berry Brothers & Rudd, Hedges & Butler, and Justerini & Brooks. Throughout the eighteenth century—and even more so in the nineteenth—such firms strove to supply the fashionable gentry. Even if wine was not originally the main business of these purveyors of fine goods, and even if spirits subsequently played a major part in their development (everyone now associates the initials of Justerini & Brooks with one of the world's most famous brands of whisky), their role in the history of great wines is not insignifiant. By popularizing the use of cylindrical bottles—sealed with a hermetic cork and easily stacked on top of one another—rather than traditional casks, they managed to convince the general public that a great wine could and should age harmoniously.

This booming trade required offices on the spot, near the vineyards, to act as brokers or dealers or both. Ambitious young businessmen who intended to buy wine for resale to merchants in England and northern Europe set up shop on the banks of the Garonne River beneath the city of Bordeaux. In the first half of the seventeenth century, the Irishmen Abraham Lawton and Tom Barton both founded dynasties devoted to great vintages which survive to this day. They were rapidly followed by other Irish, English, German and Scandinavian families, such as Cruse, Lynch, Johnston, Sichel, Schroeder & Schÿler, and Kressmann. A few Frenchmen, notably de Luze and Calvet, contrived to become members of this highly exclusive club which became known as the Chartrons, from the name of the quay and neighborhood where their firms did business (which in turn derived their name from a Carthusian monastery that stood there in medieval times).

Up until 1974, when a resounding scandal rocked them to their foundations, the Chartrons exercised a virtual monopoly over the market for great wines. Together with the estate owners—nobility or bourgeoisie—with whom they worked, these exclusive merchants effectively launched the modern concept of great wines, founded on the individual qualities of a specific vineyard and sanctified by the magic of a name.

Bordeaux's prosperity rested for many years on its special relationship with England and on its activities as a port. The port of Bordeaux (*above*) received traffic not only by sea but also from the whole of southwestern France, and was thronged with scows or flat-bottomed boats that sailed down the Dordogne laden with goods and wines from Cahors and Fronton—wines which could not be consumed locally, but had to be sold to foreign merchants. Such discriminatory practices also affected, up to the nineteenth century, wines from Libourne, which were of little interest to local traders in Bordeaux. Today the port's main business is still founded on wines from the banks of the Garonne and Gironde Rivers—Graves, Sauternes, Médoc, Bourg and Blaye. *Right*: Painted china featuring various estates in the Bordeaux region.

WHAT'S IN A NAME?

The name of an estate is not always linked solely to a merchant's decision or the owner's origins. Frequently it derives from a place-name that has over the centuries become the synonymous with the vineyard as a whole. Sometimes, the names of a number of separate and well-defined vineyards share almost identical roots. Thus Mouton-Rothschild, Lafite and Cos d'Estournel, three of the most famous estates in Médoc, derive their names from the same word, expressed in three different languages: Mouton derives directly from the old French *mothon*, meaning a mound of earth; Lafite is a deformation of "the hill" in English; while *cos* is the Gascon word for hill. As each of these vineyards came into single ownership, the owner respected its origins and merely added his own name.

As some Bordeaux estates grew in fame, so many others took inspiration from their glorious example. Féret's *Bordeaux et ses Vins*, a 2,000-page directory originally published in 1846, now lists some 7,900 vineyards in the Bordeaux region, including no fewer than sixteen with the word *Lafite* in their name, sometimes spelled with one "f" and two "ts" or two "fs" and two "ts." Similarly, Latours are legion (usually in two words, La Tour), as are calculated homages to Haut-Brion, Cheval-Blanc and Belair. In Bordeaux in particular, every vineyard, whether intentionally or not, is rooted in history, bearing witness to both a time and a place marked by specific social customs and people of influence.

Occasionally, a name may resonate like a tribute. Château Ausone, the most private of great Bordeaux wines—a villa hidden among trees overlooking the slopes of Saint-Émilion—adopted the name of the Latin poet Ausonius who owned a vineyard in the area. The debate still raging over whether Auso-nius's vineyard stood on the exact spot occupied by today's Château Ausone is beside the point, as the name has come to stand for that subtlest of links between the art of wine-making and the art of poetry.

The relationship between the vineyard's history and its name may also bear witness to a more recent past. For example, the history of Bordeaux wines has been marked by the difficulty of bequeathing an estate to a sole descendent. The ill-advises dealings of some families and the numerous offspring of others have resulted in the subdivision of properties over the centuries. Formerly vast domains have been split into two, three or four estates that nevertheless provide connoisseurs with subtle clues as to their family ties. A great, stony plateau between Saint-Émilion and Libourne is home to some of the finest vineyards producing Saint-Émilion and Pomerol wines. Under the Ancien Régime, Château Figeac was the major estate in this celebrated region. Sadly, its owners in the early nineteenth century made swift work of squandering their huge holdings. The widowed "Dame de Figeac", Félicité de Gères, was able to meet her debts only by selling off more than half her land, little by little. There thus sprang up a vineyard dubbed, naturally enough, Petit-Figeac and, beginning in 1832, another destined to become even more famous, Cheval-Blanc. Having no famous château to link with this new estate, the owners simply gave it the name by which the plot was traditionally known.

Some forty miles to the west of the plateau of Saint-Émilion, Saint-Julien produces the most consistently high-quality wine in all of Médoc. It numbers only seventeen estates, but eleven of these were officially rated *grands crus* in 1855! Three of them partly share the same name: Léoville-Barton, Léoville-Poyferré and Léoville-Las Cazes. In the eighteenth cen-

Pétrus—just Pétrus, without the ubiquitous "Château"— is unique in the Bordeaux region. A vineyard of just a dozen hectares (thirty acres) located in Pomerol, the most outlying of Bordeaux's prestigious appellations, Pétrus is the perfect reflection of a singular appellation with neither glamorous châteaux nor classified vintages. It was the owner of Pétrus, Madame Loubat, who built up the vineyard's reputation in the 1940s and 1950s, with the help of an inspired dealer, Jean-Pierre Moueix. The Moueix family now owns this outstanding vineyard, composed almost solely of clay and planted exclusively with Merlot grapes, and has made it the most famous, most expensive wine in the world—even though its initial sale price (restricted, alas, to a few selected buyers) is hardly excessive in view of the feverish speculation that now surrounds every good year.

tury, Blaise Antoine Alexandre de Gasq played an enthusiastic part in the impressive movement to provide a modern footing for Médoc, the most famous wine-growing region in the world. Through marriage, he became the owner of an estate in Saint-Julien, to which he gave the name of the Gasq family seat, Léoville, located in the neighboring province of Saintonge. Blaise de Gasq's lack of heirs and the events of the French Revolution put an end to the sole ownership of the domain as a whole, but fifty years later three proprietors contrived to enshrine the new situation for posterity. Hugh Barton, the Marquis de Lascazes, and the Baronne de Poyferré de Cère accordingly attached their own names to the new Léovilles.

Few traditional wine-growing regions have been able to take advantage of their owners' fierce determination to stand out from the crowd to such an extent. But Bordeaux vineyards had been the property of France's legal and administrative aristocracy and then, after the Revolution, of its grand bourgeoisie; the vineyards of Bordeaux could boast a few extravagant egos. The vieyards of Burgundy, by contrast, were the work of the church and the peasantry, so the source of fame became the land itself, rather than the owner. Originally the property of great aristocratic families and monastic orders, the Burgundian vineyards were sold off by the state during the Revolution and divided up between many small owners. Hence the vineyards were linked to neither a personality nor a château, so Burgundy-lovers now wax ecstatic over the names of specific plots and *climats*—the term used to describe differently exposed parcels within each vineyard. A rural municipality such as Vosne-Romanée, which indisputably produces some of the most famous wines in Burgundy, boasts forty-six hectares (110 acres) of vines classed as *premier cru*, making it the cream of the crop in an official hierarchy composed of only three grades: *cru*, *premier cru* and *grand cru*. Now, forty-six hectares is the size of a middling estate in Médoc, or even very middling, when compared to the sixty-five hectares of Latour, the seventy five of Margaux and Mouton, and the 100 of Lafite. But this does not prevent Burgundian tradition from dividing those forty-six hectares into twelve different *climats*, each bearing a name acquired centuries ago, such as Beaux Monts (in a village which has only a single slope, despite the plural "mounts"), Chaumes, Aux Reignots, Aux Malconsorts (and above it, logically enough, Au-dessus des Malconsorts). All these plots are intertwined, generating Burgundy's complicated grammar. And this syntax is further complicated by the fact that all these names are then conjugated with those of the dozens of growers who produce wine from them. Just as sailors give names to all the rocks that rise above coastal seas at low tide, so Burgundian vinegrowers have given verbal expression to the time and labor devoted to each stretch of land, and to their intimate knowledge of the area. Hence some names refer to the nature of soil, such as Aux Cras and Les Crais, which lie in chalky (*crayeux*) areas, and Chaillerts and Caillererts, which stand on ground that is *caillouteux*, or pebbly.

Sometimes, it is impossible to resist inventing plays on these evocative names: *Les Amoureuses* ("enamored ladies"), for instance,

Whereas Médoc is dotted with towers, country homes, lofty facades and impressive colonnades, in Burgundy "châteaux" are far rarer, both architecturally and in the sense of self-contained wine estates producing wines of a single appellation. Château de Pommard, with its twenty hectares (48 acres) of vines and its 40,000 bottles annually of great château wine, is one of the rare exceptions to this rule. Even Clos Vougeot (*left*), despite its massive appearance, was never a lordly residence, but rather a Cistercian monastery and then, gradually, the symbolically charged meeting place of the Confrérie du Taste-vin (the Confraternity of the Tasting Cup) which has initiated thousands of connoisseurs into the secrets of Burgundy's great wines. *Following pages*: The most famous wine in Burgundy, Romanée-Conti, comes from a single domain which also produces other pearls such as a Montrachet and a Romanée-St. Vivant.

clearly delight the famous town of Chambolle-Musigny with their *Charmes*, perhaps directed toward the *Beaux Bruns* ("dark, handsome lads")—all three of them practically touching one another in this famous village!

STYLE MAKES THE CHÂTEAU

The primacy of land over owners in Burgundy is reflected in its residences. It is rare to see ostentatiously lavish buildings, and when they do exist, they do not necessarily indicate that the owner has striven to make a wine superior to all others. You may spy historic fortresses and centuries-old country houses from afar, but their wines have never been much to speak of, while, in the village of Vosne-Romanée, it is extremely hard to spot the modest if handsome Burgundian dwelling where the supremely famous Romanée-Conti wines are made.

Exactly the opposite is true of Bordeaux, especially Médoc, where the owners' determination to set their personal stamp on their vineyards took an extraordinarily ambitious turn in the nineteenth century, going far beyond the mere name itself. Whereas the eighteenth century was characterized by the rage for planting vines in Médoc, in the nineteenth owners were seized with a passion for building. The most dazzling illustration of this frenetic period is undoubtedly Cos d'Estournel, a prestigious vineyard of Bordeaux's most westerly wine region, Saint-Estèphe. The estate ows its name to the site, Cos (formerly spelled Caux), combined with that of the founder of the vineyard, Louis-Gaspard d'Estournel. At the age of twenty-nine Louis-Gaspard, the son of a minor aristocratic family from Quercy, inherited a country estate opposite Château Lafite. He quickly decided to turn it into a brilliant rival, if not the equal, of its

"I learned to appreciate most of all that 'aristocracy of the cork' whose titles are almost always authentic and who play a modern role in modern society, a modest but specific role. France's nobility has been out of a job ever since the Tuileries Palace burned down; but the cellars of Bordeaux are eternal, and our royal wine has the power to ennoble the families who serve it." Nothing has changed since 1928, when François Mauriac wrote these lines as a preface to *Préséances*. Except perhaps that modesty is no longer in fashion. *Above*: Château Cos d'Estournel in Saint-Estèphe. *Right*: Château Margaux. *Following pages*: *A Bordeaux Architect's Dream*, painting by Carl Laubin, which notably features Haut-Brion, Léoville-Las Cazes, Latour and Margaux, among others.

famous neighbor, devoting the whole of his long life—he died in 1853 at the age of ninety-one—and above all his entire fortune to satisfying this consuming ambition. As Cos had no reputation, Louis-Gaspard had to convince the merchants of his day in the same way as gifted, ambitious wine-growers do today. He constantly enlarged his estate, buying the best plots and eliminating the weaker ones from his final selection, and invested untold sums in equipment and cellars, monitoring and checking every stage in the creation of his wine with extraordinary zeal. To these expenses he added another even more extravagant investment, guaranteed to win an international reputation in record time: using the fact that the Chartrons traders had shipped some of his two most interesting vintages to rich clients in India as his unlikely pretext, he built—in the heart of Médoc, a mere forty miles from Bordeaux—a palace with all the appearance of a fairytale pagoda.

Bruno Prats, the current owner, likes to quote Stendhal's description, penned when he was traveling through Médoc: "I rather think it is a wine-cellar... This highly elegant building, a brilliant light yellow in color, is in truth of no style; it is neither Greek, nor Gothic, but it is very gay and would seem to be rather Chinese in taste. On the facade is written a single word: Cos." The exuberant construction does not, indeed, house the dwelling quarters of the master of the estate, but rather the wine-cellars. Like its builder, Louis-Gaspard, it is wholly dedicated to the exacting passion for wine. Although its eccentricity has never been matched, it has inspired more than one aspirant to viticultural fame: hundreds of vineyard owners in Médoc built their own "châteaux" in the course of that romantic but commercially-minded century. The buildings range from the sober and classic country house in traditional Bordelais style, whether flat-fronted (as at Lynch-Bages) or U-shaped (as at Ducru-Beaucaillou), to the "little Versailles" of Beychevelle (built in the eighteenth century) or the charming turrets of Palmer and Pichon-Longueville-Comtesse de Lalande.

This frenzy of building came to a halt during the first three quarters of the twentieth century as a result of the financial difficulties experiencesd by the owners, but the new golden age which gripped Bordeaux in the 1980s saw the revival of a flamboyant tradition. The two most magnificent examples are without doubt the barrel-shaped wine-cellar at Lafite, designed by Ricardo Bofill, and the monumental renovation of Château Pichon-Longueville

The international success of Bordeaux wines in the 1980s, combined with the arrival of new owners able to invest considerable sums of money, profoundly changed ways of working vines and wines in Bordeaux, and perhaps had even more effect on the region's external appearance. Never since the golden age of the mid-nineteenth century have architects been so solicited, stone-cutters so prized, masons, carpenters and painters so sought-after, manufacturers of wine-producing equipment so courted. Virtually the entire Bordeaux area has become a permanent construction site, with estates in a constant state of building, rebuilding and improvement. In this regard, the prize must go to Château Pichon–Baron de Longueville, entirely revamped and "reconceived" in a quasi-pharaonic style (*above*).

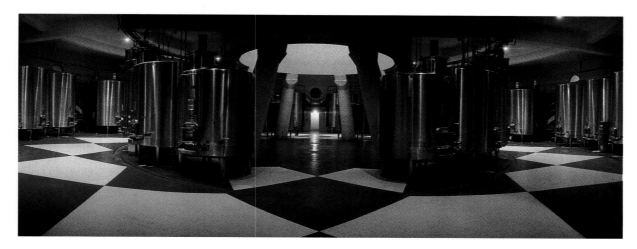

devised by Patrick Dillon and Jean de Gastines.

Indeed, the architecture of its winemaking buildings can play a significant role in establishing the specific image of an estate. Every region therefore cultivates it own style, often inspired by local tradition. A photograph of virtually any South African estate, for example, will show vines with red autumn foliage, behind which there rises an elegant white building topped by a dark band. This silhouette is typical of the original houses built by the region's white population in Cape Dutch style, with white-washed walls, a rounded gable over the central door bearing the family coat of arms and date of construction, and a thatched roof. Proud of these houses, the South Africans look after them with care, regularly renovating the rooms, renewing the thatch, keeping the walls a dazzling white, and generally turning them into little paradises of blue skies, pink bougainvillea and lush green vegetation. The Dutch, for whom the Cape was a perfect stopping point on the route to the East Indies in the seventeenth century, imported their architecture along with their national customs. It is said that the gables, which generally contain only a single window to light the attic, was where slaves were hidden when enemy ships landed.

Nowadays, most newcomers to the wine business build perfect imitations of the Cape Dutch style: more than just a relic of history, architecture here is a strong tradition indicating a level of skill and a respect for the local soil and climate. The few exceptions to this rule include the Vergelegen estate, where the magnificent underground cellar is modeled on the one at Château Lafite.

In other countries, traditionalism is out of place. Chile, for example, is a major new winemaking frontier where it is more important to display the image of an ultra-dynamic vineyard in a state of constant revolution and continual growth. In a booming wine "industry," the most ambitious players do not hesitate to sink millions of dollars in projects that may seem incredible. One rich owner, for instance, a great lover of horses as well as wine, commissioned a huge fermenting room in the shape of a horse shoe (the Pirque stables outside Santiago).

A Norwegian businessman, who moved to Chile years ago is meanwhile making his dream come true: on the *fundo* where he grows fruit, has behives and raises horses from his native land, he has planted a vineyard and constructed a highly unusual winery. The architect is his own son, and this is his first project. The fermenting room is in raw

Countless estates have improved their winemaking facilities, from new fermenting rooms at Domaine de Chevalier, Mission Haut-Brion, Château Branaire, and Château Pichon-Baron de Longueville (*above*) to refurnished wine cellars at Château Lafite, Château d'Yquem, and Château Cos d'Estournel, to name but a few. Apart from their carefully groomed esthetic impact, these changes have also propelled many great Bordeaux vintages to the cutting edge of winemaking technology, at a time when the initiative seemed to be shifting to America and Australia. With their phalanxes of oenologists monitoring and advising on the winemaking process, some major estates briefly ran the risk of forgetting the quality of vine and grape. More recent investments have therefore focused on vineyard rather than cellar—everything ultimately depends on the grape.

concrete, with wooden roofbeams supporting a copper roof. The overall shape of the inner structure is supposed to represent a ship—the curved office is placed in the "bow," and top-hit by a hatch similar to those found in sailing ships. No detail has been overlooked—from the stainless steel cellar doors to the lamps especially imported from Japan to light the reception area for the harvest—in an effort to demonstrate both the owner's munificence and his desire to create the greatest wine possible.

Finally, features specific to each country must also be taken into account. Thus two Frenchmen—Paul Pontallier, director of Château Margaux, and Bruno Prats, owner of Cos d'Estournel—have set up a small Bordeaux-style estate, Vina Aquitania, at the foot of the Andes. Local color is not the issue here: in the cellars the vats are set on a thick concrete foundations but loosely anchored so that they can sway without toppling over—during the many earthquakes that punctuate life in the area, vats fixed too rigidly would crumple like a crushed aluminum can.

THE PRESTIGE OF A LABEL

Having a name is one thing. Making it known is another. And one of the best advertising mediums remains the bottle and its label. Here producers have the opportunity to display as much originality and personality as they wish, even if very few wine-growers know how to take advantage of it with true imagination and flair. For every Philippe de Rothschild who combines the art of winemaking with art pure and simple by transforming the Mouton-Roth-

Houses and châteaux on wine estates can also make delightful places to live. Californian owners have put their concern for lifestyle to good use by designing estates in which cellars, offices and living quarters are combined with charm and efficiency (*above:* Clos Pegase, Calistoga, Napa Valley). In other regions with older traditions, such as the famous Afrikaner farms in South Africa, buildings naturally incorporate both residential and agricultural functions (*right:* the Boschendal estate in Franschoek, near Cape Town). The estates in Médoc are devoted primarily to promoting their image (with a few exceptions such as Château Léoville-Barton and Château Talbot), although this is not the case elsewhere in France.

schild label into an extraordinary gallery of contemporary painting and illustration, there are countless other producers whose bottles are lamentably ordinary or downright ugly.

Baron Philippe de Rothschild, who more than anyone has an added artistic—even god-like—dimension to winemaking, devoted his entire life to the magnificent Mouton estate, purchased by the Rothschild family in the nineteenth century. When he inherited the property in 1922, it was rated only a *second cru* in the official (and still valid) classification of Bordeaux vineyards established in 1855. He spared no pains in the vineyards, in the cellars and in the world at large in order to make Mouton the equal of the *premiers crus*, a distinction that it was finally awarded by ministerial decree in 1973. To emphasize the artistic value of the wine and the unique quality of each vintage, in 1945 Baron Philippe conceived the idea, of asking a different celebrity from the art world every year to create an original work for the upper part of the label. From Picasso to film-director John Huston, some of the greatest names of the twentieth century have thereby contributed to the glory of Mouton while also, along the way, sparking the enthusiasm of collectors.

The label also has a role to play when it comes to more modest wines, offering a tantalizing hint of treasures to be discovered, as witnessed by a story from Chile, at the foot of the Andes. The Chileans are true professionals when it comes to exporting, whether they are dealing in mineral products such as copper, in fruit, or in wine. A great deal of their wine output is exported to the United States, Asia, the Uni-

ted Kingdom and other European countries. All products destined for export are assessed and selected with greater care than those for domestic consumption. Once Chilean consumers cottoned on to this fact, they began to equate export with quality—an association shrewdly exploited by certain labels. The most fashionable wine on the list at Santa Rita in Santiago, one of the finest *bodegas* (restaurants) in the country, is a *Casa Real exportacion*, as though the wine were intended for export.

Chilean supermarkets, meanwhile, stock some of the many wines from Concha y Toro, the country's largest wine producer, whose wines range from the best to the worst. The latter, selling at under two dollars, bears one of the simplest labels in the world: no château, no setting sun, no flowers, no varietal name, no vintage year. Just a stamp, like those used on wooden shipping crates, saying in large letters "*Exportacion.*" Though the contents are barely drinkable, the word and the dream it evokes still sell.

Finally, other producers mark their originality through the appearance of their bottles. Everywhere in the world, an Italian pot-bellied bottle half-covered with woven raffia is associated with Chianti. And in many countries the flat, flask-like bottle of rosé is synonymous with the sweet and refreshing pleasure of Mateus wine from Portugal. Bordeaux wines —and by extension all those made from Cabernet or Merlot grapes—are recognizable by their tall, cylindrical bottle, while German and Alsatian whites—as well as most Rieslings and Gewürztraminers the world over—also have their own long slender silhouette.

"As years flow by / they fashion / works, life, wine"—Philippe de Rothschild. Few gallery owners can claim to have exhibited original works by contemporary artists as diverse and as celebrated as Picasso, Chagall, Cocteau, Dali, Francis Bacon, and film-director John Huston. Every year Baron de Rothschild, succeeded now by his daughter Philippine, commisiones a different artist to illustrate the label for the new vintage of Château Mouton Rothschild. *Above*: The sixty-fourth and penultimate vintage bottled by the baron before his death in 1987, bearing a painting by Bernard Séjourné. *Following pages*: Rare wines: a demi-john of Eszencia (*left*), made solely from *aszu* grapes with "noble rot," with such a high level of sugar that it looks like a thick liqueur and may age for several centuries; and a bottle well over a hundred years old of one of the most famous Spanish wines, a Marquès de Riscal Rioja (*right*).

VICTORIA
HEREDEROS DEL
ARQUÉS DE RISCA
ELCIEGO (ALAVA
1875
CONCEDIDA. MARQUE DEPOSÉE. TRADE MARK. SCHÜTZ MARKE
PHILOMATHIQUE
XIIIe EXPOSITION
BORDEAUX
NATIONALE, INTERNATIONALE, UNIVERSELLE
DIPLÔME D'HONNEUR
1895

THE CLAMOR OF CHAMPAGNE

Clearly, the purpose of elaborating and bottling a wine is to enable the public to enjoy it. For centuries, producers and merchants have vied with one another in devising ways of encouraging as many wine lovers as possible to know and appreciate their products. For any given type of wine—champagne, for example—this ambition may take very different forms. In the Champagne region itself, major firms such as Pommery in Reims and Deutz in Aÿ encourage tourists to visit the labyrinthine caves hollowed out of the limestone where their wines are aged. Here visitors are introduced to the principal stages in the making of champagne: the fermenting room, the bottling operation, storage, disgorging by

hand or machine, capping, labeling, and so on.

Every firm has its own style. At the Roederer premises in Reims, the wooden casks in which blended wines are put to age inspire respect. At Castellane, meanwhile, presenting a number of museums, ranging in subject from labels to wine and onto—butterflies, fascinate both connoisseurs and their children. On the Avenue de Champagne, Epernay's main street, Mercier offers a flashy, hour-long show retracing the life of Eugène Mercier, whose inspired advertising made champagne famous throughout the world. The show begins with a film crammed light and music—fireworks, popping champagne corks, a grand human epic played out to the ringing strains of a brass band. It then moves to a glass-sided elevator which slowly sinks down to the cellars, a descent of some twenty yards or so, lined with statues and extravagant decorative features carved out of the living rock. Once at the bottom, visitors are led to a little train such as might be found in an amusement park, which follows a laser beam through the broad galleries embellished with sculptures on historical subjects carved in the limestone. Finally, visitors enter a gigantic room densely packed with gifts and gadgets: books on the firm and its great founder, gift assortments of bottles, chocolates, cups, plates, posters, tee-shirts and of course individual bottles of champagne. The whole extravaganza ends with a tasting.

At the other end of the avenue, Moët & Chandon choose to devote more time to the actual making of champagne. Numerous guides—speaking eight different languages—explain the process point by point as visitors travel along the cool, damp corridors. Although Mercier and Moët & Chandon are now owned by the same corporation, their different status images are cultivated even in these organized tours, based on popular entertainment for the former, and sophisticated connoisseurship for the latter.

Champagne producers were among the first members in the wine trade to make advertising and publicity a major part of their development. Starting in the second half of the nineteenth century, poster artists produced on countless designs for champagne firms, most frequently combining the allegorical figure of a shapely woman with a bottle brimming with bubbles or bunches of ripe, luscious grapes. In the early twentieth century, some brands singled themselves out by opting for elegance, finesse and distinction rather than images of abundance. Labels already played an essential role, mobilizing an ingenious range of pretexts for "special vintages" (*above*), as is still the practice today. *Right*: Detail from an allegorical carving at the Mercier firm in Épernay.

Outside of its original zone of production, champagne's mission to make itself loved can sometimes take a much less restrained turn. In the United States, champagne bars bearing names such as the Bubble Lounge or Le Flute take champagne-cult to absurd limits. The origins of the latest fad, which involves drinking this noble wine through a straw, are unclear. Some claim that during a New York fashion show a major designer offered his models straws to preserve their lipstick when sipping their champagne. When it was reported in the fashionable press, the idea took off. Then came the nicknames: Krazy Krug (Krug being considered the champagne of somewhat stuffy connoisseurs up to that point) and Taitt' for Two, intended to encourage lovers to sip Taittinger champagne eye to eye. This minor vogue (for not all Americans drink their champagne this way) paid off for the Bubble Lounge, packed on New Year's Eve with revellers drinking in the new year by sipping half-bottles of champagne through a straw.

This brief world tour of the fame of champagne concludes in South Africa, a country that has opened up to tourism since the abolition of apartheid in 1991. Its wine world is no exception, and the wine route taking in the estates of the Cape region is not only to be recommended but also very well organized. In places it is quite magnificent, as at Vergelegen, where the entire vineyard can be visited. Located near Sommerset West and the sea, this immense estate is flanked by mountains and boasts a range of farming activities (including several hundred head of cattle, and endless orchards of apricot and peach trees alongside the vines). Tours leave at set times and last a good two hours, taking visitors by bus to the wine-cellar, half-buried on top of a hill, where each stage of the winemaking process is explained in detail, with the aid of frequent references to French practice. The guide explains encouragingly that both grape varieties and casks come from Bordeaux, and that Cape champagnes, although renamed Cape Classic sparkling wine at France's request, are indeed true champagnes—well-calculated remarks which certainly seem reassuring—to judge by visitors' expressions—to serve as an effective sales pitch. Even despite itself, and even in the Antipodes, champagne still cultivates its unique image!

SELLING WINE

These numerous strategies, whether international or not, are clearly all aimed at a single goal: selling wine, and preferably at the highest possible price. Although no one would challenge the fundamental necessity of this part of the operation, it does not always go smoothly. The alcoholic content of wine exposes the fears that men harbor regarding their own weaknesses, and spurs the codes of practice they lay down for self-regulation.

In most countries, happily, the wine trade contrives to project an image combining the picturesque and the respectable. One of the most beguiling examples of this may be seen, without doubt, in the image presented by traditional Paris wine merchants for over a century. Their shops acquire an inimitable charm from their dark marble store-fronts inscribed with Belle-Époque style gold lettering proclaiming the name of the firm and promising *vins fins* and other *liqueurs*, their large window dis-

The names for different bottle sizes vary between champagne or wine (*above*: the label of one of the most famous champagnes, Dom Pérignon, produced by Moët & Chandon) and other wines. In Champagne, a magnum contains the equivalent of two standard bottles, or 1.5 liters; a jeroboam, 3 liters; a rehoboam, 4.5 liters; a methuselah, 6 liters; a salmanazar, 9 liters; a balthazar, 12 liters; and, finally, a nebuchadnezzar, 15 liters (the equivalent of 20 bottles). For all other wines, the Bordeaux system applies: a magnum contains 1.5 liters, a marie-jeanne, 2.5 liters; a double magnum, 3 liters; a jeroboam, 5 liters; and an imperial, 6 liters. *Following pages*: A selection of wines from California, South Africa, Italy, Austria, Spain and New Zealand, displayed at the Paris wine merchant Caves Augé.

plays bursting with bottles, carefully arranged and hand-labeled in italic script, their solid-wood shelves with a smooth patina of age, their aromas of wax and wood, their assistants clad in full-length whose white aprons descend to their shoes, and the professional advice they offer.

Until just a few years ago, these neighborhood wine merchants—now fewer and fewer in number in the face of competition from the large retail chains—boasted a surprising and unforgettable standard-bearer in the person of Jean-Baptiste Besse, who had a modest store in one of the oldest and most picturesque quarters of Paris, the Sainte-Geneviève hill not far from the Sorbonne. Originally from the rural region of Corrèze, Besse was a wily but generous character whose customers for many years knew affectionately as "old Besse." On entering his premises, visitors were confronted merely with stacks of ordinary wine, blandly overseen by Besse. This was because customers had to prove their worth before the true nature of the establishment was revealed to them.

After several visits, you might begin to get a little impatient, wondering whether the treasures for which the place was reputed were nothing more than a lure. Only then would old Besse agree to take you down to his cellar, a veritable Aladdin's cave. From the entrance steps to the furthest corners of this two-storey cellar dating from the Middle Ages, the gloom would slowly reveal uneven heaps of dusty bottles, apparently piled up at random. As Besse described a wine, explaining the soil, the climate and the people that had produced

it, you would find yourself transported from the hill of Sainte-Geneviève to the cellar of a château in Bordeaux or an estate in Burgundy. Besse and his cellar summed up the true art of a real wine merchant—transmitting knowledge, enthusiasm, and a unique emotion.

It is an art that has now been exported all across the globe. Whether in the United States, Japan or Europe, a wine merchant remains someone with skilled knowledge, an interpreter who can advise without intimidating, who can communicate enthusiasm and a shared quest for pleasure. These multiple talents are also displayed by good wine stewards and, less frequently, by restaurateurs. The job of wine steward is an old one: the households of gourmet aristocrats would include a man —or several— acquainted with the secrets of the cellar who was responsible for serving wine during meals. Two hundred years ago, guests would not have dreamed of pouring wine from the bottle themselves. The wealth and complexity of the choice of wines available has now made the job of choosing and pouring it one of the haughtiest in a restaurant.

For over a century, fine restaurants featured men of serious (if sometimes ruddy) mien, stiff bearing, and somber dress, who with a masterful gesture would repeatedly refill the diners' glasses. These traditional stewards, who always wore a chain around their neck as though to signify membership of some secret confraternity, viewed themselves more as guardians of the temple of wine than as pioneers of new discoveries and pleasures; indeed it is said that the wine steward at the famous

Above: The method for making *Eiswein* is one of the most original of any wine in the world. These German or Austrian wines are literally "ice wines" as the grapes are picked very late, often in December, when the fruit has already been frozen by continental Europe's sharp winters. The grapes are then pressed immediately, without being warmed in any way, for much of the water contained in the fruit is transformed into ice crystals, which remain in the press as the sweet, liquid juice runs off. This produces wines that are very high in sugar, yet with much greater acidity and vivacity than wines made in classic fashion from late-picked grapes or fruit attacked by "noble rot."

Paris restaurant Le Grand Véfour in the 1950s would serve his customers with just one red wine, always from a carafe, regardless of the dish ordered: a Château Lynch-Bages!

A new generation of wine stewards, or sommeliers, in France and especially in Japan, Germany, Italy, and the United States, has totally revolutionized the profession's style and methods. Nowadays, it is fashionable to try to get customers off the beaten track of Bordeaux wines without overly upsetting them, advising them in light of the dishes they have ordered, and suggesting a range of wines that can be sampled without breaking the bank. This is no cause for complaint, since today's sommeliers are better at their jobs and necessarily more familiar with the whole range of wines. Every four years an international contest crowns The World's Best Sommelier, a veritable Renaissance man of wine. After a long period of French domination, the most recent winners have been Japanese and German...

DRANSY.

The Nicolas firm was one of the few French companies specializing in the marketing of wines. This it did with remarkable commercial dynamism, notably by inviting famous artists to illustrate the catalog of fine wines it offered to customers at the end of every year. It owed its enormous pre-war success, however, to an invented mascot called Nectar, putative son of a Nicolas wine merchant, a likeable dolt with a slight tendency to overindulge his penchant for a tipple, yet who conscientiously carried out the firm's deliveries. As appealing as Nectar may have been, Nicolas subsequently encountered some difficulty in freeing itself from his image, which seemed less reminiscent of sophisticated appreciation of wine than of a drinking song from Alfred Jarry's *Ubu Rex*: "Bloated face, trembling hand / are the drunkard's just due. / So hurrah for Poland / and good old Ubu!"

The
Pleasure
of
Wine Tasting

In his novel *Uranus*, Marcel Aymé decribed with his characteristic biting irony the tragic character of a bistro owner who during the German Occupation was more of a drunk than a traitor (although for the latter he was shot), noting that "like every good Frenchman" he drank twelve liters of wine per day. A habit such as this clearly has little to do with delight and even less with taste. But if this type of excess has often been taken to represent—both in literature and, alas, real life—the ultimate image of human degeneration, when wine is good it has a far greater capacity to convey the most subtle of sensations. And while moderation is obviously a necessary precondition for the full expression of this pleasure, so is wine's ability to be "good."

This talent is far from being self-evident, as we have seen throughout the preceding chap-

ters. No grape is programmed to be transformed into a fine wine. Only occasionally does the alchemy occur—and when it does, the results may be dazzling. In *The Great Vintage Wine Book*, the British wine writer Michael Broadbent used the following terms to describe his impressions of a 1945 Mouton-Rothschild, a wine considered by many great tasters as the finest of the century: "A Churchill of a wine... It has a magnificent, deep, almost opaque appearance, ruby with a pronounced mahogany rim; fabulous and, I like to think, totally unmistakable bouquet—highly concentrated, intense blackcurrant Cabernet Sauvignon aroma, touch of cinnamon. And flavor to match. Ripe, rich yet with the body and component parts to keep it in balance for years to come!"

Few drinks, indeed few foods, are likely to inspire such admiration. Yet apart from a touch of lyricism due to such a monumental wine, Broadbent analyzes it in the customary fashion of his profession. First he describes its color, known in French as the *robe*, stressing on its density and its dark but lively hue, an unmistakable sign of health and vigor. As wine evolves in the bottle, its ruby color will take on mahogany highlights, or amber ones if it was originally golden. Retaining such a vigourous hue is therefore a prodigious feat. Then he describes the bouquet. Tasters also speak of a wine's "nose," as they hold the glass under their own. Broadbent praises its perfume, the complex and intense blend of aromas that recalls the scent of fruit, cinnamon and spices, which are in fact the fragrances most commonly associated with the main variety of grape used in this wine. Finally, examining the wine in the mouth, the taster assesses its density and texture, as a gourmet would when tasting a special dish. A wine may be soft and smooth, or on the contrary rich and robust, which is the case here. And yet, notes Broadbent, the overall effect is an inspiring sensation

Above: The year 1945—"Year of Victory"—was perhaps the vintage of the century for Bordeaux wines, as heralded in indisputable fashion by Mouton Rothschild. The cult of great vintages goes back to long before the twentieth century, however, for as early as Roman times certain wines from great years were laid down with care. And woe betide, then as now, any unfortunate who, like the young hero—named Pétrus!—of Alexandre Dumas's novel *Les Mohicans de Paris*, does not accord due respect to a precious vintage, as pointed out by his indignant uncle: "What, wretch! I pour you a glass of Haut-Laffitte [sic], the very one laid down in 1812, the year of the comet [in fact, 1811], wine worth twelve francs in my cellar but which, once warmed and served at the right temperature, is priceless, and you drink this wine with water!" *Right*: Three prestigious French wines: a Château Coutet (Sauternes-Barsac), a Château Beychevelle (Saint-Julien), and a Vieilles Vignes vintage Chambolle-Musigny from Domaine Grivelet.

of finesse and elegance. These three factors—sight, smell and taste—all contribute to the taster's unequivocal conclusions.

Michael Broadbent is not merely a specialist in great wines but also an auctioneer at Christie's which, like its rival Sotheby's, mounts extravagant auctions of "claret, port and other fine wines." He is thus also an principal player in the remarkable circuit that sends great bottles from one continent to another in order to satisfy the passion and fill the cellars of the world's greatest connoisseurs.

COLLECTORS AND ENTHUSIASTS

A few guests wearing tuxedos and evening gowns prepare to enter an elegant house in an affluent suburb of Singapore. The stifling humidity outdoors is immediately replaced by the uniform coolness of air-conditioning. The house, like almost all the buildings in this city-state, is of recent date and of no particular charm. The vestibule, which serves as a foyer, and the large drawing- and dining room are soberly decorated in a style combining Western furniture with the subtleties of Chinese interior decoration. Nothing could seem more unexceptional until you discover what lies behind a reinforced steel door.

Behind this door our hosts, a Chinese surgeon and his wife, have installed an immense container wholly devoted to the cult of great wines. In this hermetically sealed space, a cool and constant temperature is maintained by an air conditioner even more powerful than those

that cool the rest of the house. A humidifier, meanwhile, maintains a high level of humidity. Shelves rise to the ceiling, leaving an aisle just wide enough for a man of average build to slide between them and holding a meticulously ordered and catalogued hoard of precious bottles.

The most famous names from Napa Valley and Sonoma—Mondavi, Phelps and Beaulieu Reserve—rub shoulders here with Montrachets from Burgundy and Romanée-Contis and Musignys from the Vogüé estate. A few carefully chosen Australian pearls—the greatest vintages from Grange-Hermitage—lie opposite a selection of Bordeaux *premiers crus* and the most dazzling "superseconds" (as Anglo-American brokers call the vintages ranked from second to fifth category in 1855 but whose prices now regularly approach the summits of their class, such as Léoville-Las Cases, Lynch-Bages, Cos d'Estournel and Pichon-Longueville-Comtesse de Lalande). Then come Von Schubert Rieslings, Hermitage de Chave, Côte Rôtie de Guigal, Châteauneuf-du-Pape de Rayas, Barolo de Gaja, Sassicaia —that is to say the pick of the Rhône and Rhine Valleys and the cream of the Italian crop—not to mention all the other extraordinary wines from lesser-known vineyards that have managed to rise head and shoulders above the common run. And finally, the finest vintages of prestige champagnes, from Krug to Roederer to Dom Pérignon complete the picture. All the greatest vintages of the century are aging in this cold room, cooler than a traditional underground cellar in the West, even if an expert eye soon notes that the doctor's zeal

"Ah, my Belovéd, fill the Cup that clears / To-day of past Regrets and future Tears. . . . / For some we loved, the loveliest and the best / That from his Vintage rolling Time has prest." Ten centuries after the Persian poet, free-thinker, and astronomer Omar Khayyam penned these lines (as rendered by Edward Fitzgerald), a sommelier sampling a golden Bruitenverwachting wine (*above*) and an Asian taster in Singapore assessing some of the finest Bordeaux vintages (*left*) relive the same sensations and pleasures.

for acquisition has increased significally from the early 1980s.

This athletic and energetic sexagenarian —whom we will call Dr. Yang—is a member of a private and informal international confraternity, which brings together—through their shared enthusiasm at least—the world's greatest wine lovers. The number of its members is obviously impossible to establish: all we know is that they may be encountered in almost every latitude, both in countries with a long tradition of wine drinking and in regions where the very word "wine" was barely known a mere twenty years ago.

This much we know—or rather the merchants and owners of great estates know it, for these are the customers who suddenly send prices rocketing, who corner the supply of a given year, who send the reputation of a given château into orbit. Most of them have made their money in some completely different kind of business, and discovered the delights of great wine one day through a chance encounter, visit, or tasting. For a while wine was probably a hobby as much as a means of investment, or even of speculation. And then, while others put their money on some new and ostentatious fad, from conceptual art to sport cars, they gradually became aware that the pleasure of wine is one of discovery and appreciation —constantly renewed—on both a sensual and an intellectual level. Some may not be as wealthy as others, but this consuming passion has dictated the direction of their lives, and they have organized their professional lives in such a way as to enable them to satisfy it.

Their passion takes many different forms. Dr. Yang spends several months each year in Europe, and makes regular visits to other great vineyards around the globe. Other connoisseurs rush from one auction to another, or throw the *place de Bordeaux* (as the brokers of Bordeaux are collectively known), into turmoil by scooping up some prestigious vintages before they have even been bottled. Others again specialize in old wines—vintages that President Thomas Jefferson, a great connoisseur of European wine, might have had in his cellar in the late eighteenth century—or in vintages that claim to be the best year the twentieth century: 1928, 1945, 1947, 1959, 1961, 1982, 1990. Some nurse a secret passion, opening their cellars only to close friends and family, while others, on the contrary, play on the media hullabaloo unfailingly triggered by the hosting of a huge, prestigious tasting.

The members of this exclusive confraternity—like producers, merchants and speculators—treat as their bibles the guides and publications in which professional tasters make or break reputations according to their assessment of the world's finest wines. For this world of passionate enthusiasm is also a global market, with its players, its stakes, and its referees.

MARRYING WINE TO GASTRONOMY

But let us return to our *soirée* in Singapore. Dr. Yang has selected a dozen different vintages—German, Italian, French—from his Aladdin's cave. In the tiny kitchen nearby, the hostess is busy with the three Chinese and Malay assistants who are helping her in the preparation of this evening's grand dinner. To accompany these wines—each with its own ancestral traditions, each drunk for centuries according to well-established local gastronomic customs—, our hostess has devised some astonishing compositions combining the fundamentals of French cuisine with those of Chinese gastronomy, associating a steamcooked side dish here with a roast of meat there, marrying oriental spices with the flavors of a distant land.

All great wines benefit from being decanted one to six hours prior to drinking, depending on the type (*right*, Opus One, one of the most famous Napa Valley wines, created by the American Robert Mondavi and the Frenchman Philippe de Rothschild). Contact with oxygen enhances the bouquet of such wines and allows to develop to the full their aromas. If a wine cannot withstand a few hours of contact with the open air, this indicates a vintage already suffering from a marked tendency towards oxidation. The only precaution to observe with regard to decanting, therefore, concerns very old bottles whose color is already turning to amber and whose content-level is low in the neck (the resul of evaporation, causing increased contact with oxygen). These bottles should be decanted just prior to serving, in order simply to separate the wine from any sediment that has formed in the bottle.

As the charm begins to work its spell, the guests at this gourmet dinner discover a new —and undoubtedly most profound—aspect of great wine: its ability to take on an even greater dimension in association with gastronomic pleausres, even when the cuisine originates from the opposite ends of the earth.

Thousands of miles from Dr. Yang's dining room, on the other side of the globe, in the Place de la Madeleine in Paris, the Lucas-Carton restaurant offers the bustling sight of black-suited waiters who flitting from table to table offering the best of French haute cuisine to an international clientele. In this temple of gastronomy, which he has run for nearly fifteen years, Alain Senderens is in full flood: "Call the kitchen!" He has just had a flash of inspiration. "The coriander doesn't go at all! And oven baking isn't the answer—the tannins in this wine call for something crisper. Frédéric." (to the chef), "could you do me the same thing again right away, but this time in a pan and lightly basted in acacia honey? And above all, no coriander!"

Senderens tastes and tastes again all the dishes for which he has devised countless variations. The white tablecloth is set with fine china plates and impeccably laid silver, and crowning the whole ensemble is a row of majestic glasses. Into each of these enormous, tulip-shaped glasses, the wine steward has poured a few centiliters of a different wine. Senderens sniffs them one after another, studies their color, then swirls the wine on his expert palate, before discreetly spitting the contents into an elegant receptacle specially designed for this professional purpose. After having absorbed the multifarious précis of information deciphered by his sharpened senses, he pierces tiny fragments of the masterpiece on the plate with his fork, before bringing it to his lips in a gesture tinged with impatience. He has selected the specific wine which in his view marries best with his creation. Once the choice has been made, naturally, Senderens notices that the marriage is not quite perfect—the seasoning of the dish needs to be rectified, or the garnish changed, or an ingredient eliminated. Sometimes soliciting the opinion of his chef, sometimes of his wine steward, he tries to analyze the complex relationship that develops between various tastes, aromas and colors, and between the highly disparate elements of wine and food.

Although this is not a marriage governed by scientific laws, it is nevertheless susceptible to obey a host of rules, mechanisms, and intuitions that Senderens has noted, classified and developed empirically over the years. This quest might appear vain and superficial, but it takes on another light when you consider that—for those of us with the good fortune to have enough to eat every day—a meal is one of the few occasions in the day devoted solely to pleasure. Like the thousands of gourmets who flock to his restaurant, Senderens understands how essential it is to be demanding when it comes to pleasure, and to maintain an invigorating and unflagging curiosity of mind and senses. "True gastronomy," he rants, "is the ideal marriage of the elements of a meal—the food and the wine."

In the early 1970s, Senderens was the turbulent leader of a generation of brilliant, iconoclastic chefs and one of the main pioneers of Nouvelle Cuisine, which was to do for gastronomy what the New Wave had done for cinema, rejuvenating and lightening it in a constant search for inventiveness, sometimes to excess. As the years went by and laurels accumulated, Senderens refused to be tamed and resisted the academicism that threatens all Young Turks as they grow older. Instead he continued to reflect and realized one day that he had neglected, like most chefs wrestling with their demanding art, to take sufficient

"Some unknown wine in my cellar lies / surrounded by guards. / If I wanted to drink it, why should I try? / It's not on the cards. I have no key, nor will any voice tell / if it's a wine to be dumped / or to be left long and well / before being drunk." These lines from Jean Cocteau's *Clair-Obscur* might have been inspired by Andrew Lloyd-Webber's wine cellar at Sydmonton. A great deal of talent and experience would be needed to reveal all the secrets stored here, still possessed by Serena Sutcliffe, director of the wine department at Sotheby's in London. Determining a wine's peak depends not only on a knowledge of the vineyard soil and vine stocks, the year, and the method of vinification, but also on the way the bottles have been stored, high humidity and a cool, constant temperature being the two key conditions.

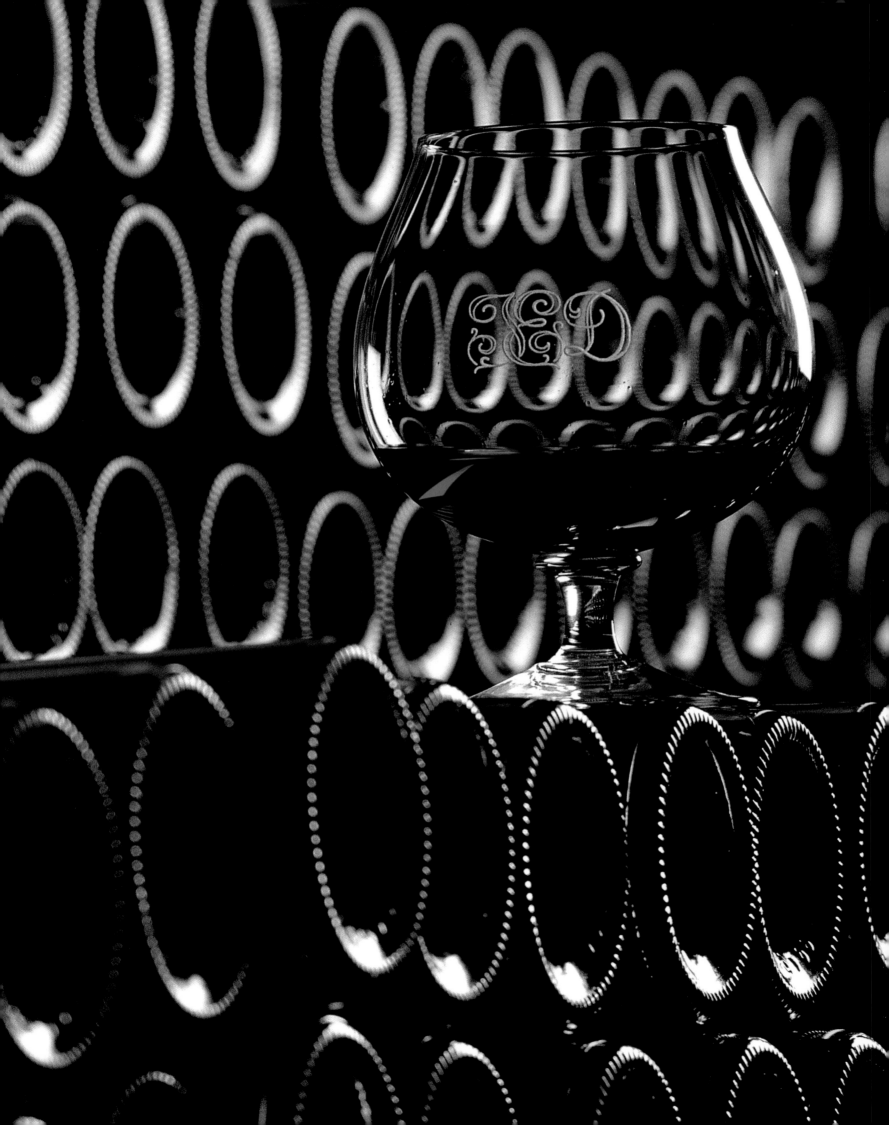

interest in the wines that accompanied the dishes he created. It was an awareness triggered by his encounter with a remarkable oenologist, Jacques Puisais.

Oenologists are generally chemists who specialize in vinification, from the study of the maturity curve of the ripening grape to the measuring of the acidity of a young wine. Curiously, many oenologists—like many restaurateurs—miss the essential point: the stimulation of sensory feelings by great wines when drunk with a meal. Puisais steadily evolved from a cold analyst of wine into an aesthete longing to understand the mysterious mechanisms governing the pleasures of taste. Together Senderens and Puisais, both scientists and gourmets, set out through countless testing sessions to establish empirically the precise flavors of wines and dishes.

How to know the right moment and appropriate circumstances for tasting wines: Californian wine merchant Kermit Lynch, one of the most discriminating of American tasters who has retained his wisdom and enthusiasm undiminished through thirty years of travelling the vineyards, offers a perfect explanation of this final requirement, which places each wine in its right time and place. Arguing that wines can only be judged in relationship to a specific context he goes on: "Take two impeccable wines, the Domaine Tempier Bandol rosé —which *The Wine Advocate* has called the finest rosé in France—and a bottle of Château Margaux, which many critics consider the finest Médoc of the day. Compare the two side by side. Award points. Do not be surprised if the Margaux wins handily. Now serve the same two wines with a boiled artichoke and rate them again. The Margaux is bitter and metallic-tasting, whereas the Bandol rosé stands up and dances like Baryshnikov.

"Which is the better wine? Which *wins*?

"Or compare a good Musigny with a good Monthelie [two Burgundies, the Musigny being famous and costly, the Monthelie more modest]. More likely than not, if the wines are well made, the Musigny will win, but your own pleasure at table would best be served by a light, spirited Monthelie with, for example, fresh egg noodles and truffles, and an older, nobler Burgundy like Musigny afterward with the proper cheeses. There you see a sensible progression of two impeccable wines. Comparing them side by side, you will find one a winner, the other a loser. Served intelligently at table, neither wine loses, your pleasure crescendos, and you, finally, are the winner.

"And those people who would always drink the Musigny over a Monthelie no matter what they have on their plate are not wine lovers. They are status seekers."

What emerges from these lines from Lynch's *Adventure on the Wine Route*—as well as from Alain Senderens' comments in Paris and Dr. Yang's demonstration in Singapore—is that a great wine only expresses its true personality when combined with food in a perfect marriage, whether at a fine restaurant or at a simple meal among friends. Then alone it will reveal all its facets, and deploying its full taste potential. The tannins which give a fabulous Cabernet wine when tasted alone an impres-

White wines (*above*, an Australian white, Grant Burge) display their best features at a temperature of 8° to 10° C (46° to 50° F). Their aromatic palette is not affected and they develop complexity and subtlety in the mouth while retaining their freshness. At higher temperatures, white wines lose freshness, while lower ones will totally paralyze the bouquet. Red wines should be served at various temperatures depending on their style. Fruity, supple wines such as Beaujolais (*left*, a Morgon from Domaine Jean Descombes) are at their best around 12° C (53° F). More structured, meatier red wines need to be served at 16° or 17° C (62° F) to express their full potential; and certain very generous wines such as Côtes du Rhône can even be served at a slightly higher temperature.

sion of power that is almost aggressive, will melt together with the dense texture of roast pigeon or the vigorous but fine texture of a fillet of beef grilled to perfection. A Sancerre —a white wine with astonishing vivacity—will refresh and sharpen the senses of anyone wise enough to combine it with a slice of dry goat's cheese on toasted country bread. A majestic Barolo with startling tannins and acidity suddenly becomes smooth and silky when associated with the tagliatelle and white truffles of which its native Piedmont is so proud.

Such examples are endless. All wines—or at least all good wines—are born to marry, some day, a festive or everyday dish, a local recipe or one from the other side of the planet, a complex composition or a simple slice of sausage. Even wines drunk as an aperitif, most notably champagne, are never better than when accompanied by a few well-chosen appetizers.

MEMORIES AND FEELINGS

The rest is up to the drinker—to you, in the privacy of your own cellar and dinner table. The cellar steps are all the more treacherous if your mind is preoccupied on the way down. The still-vague idea of the precise wine to be drunk at dinner suddenly becomes a unique and fundamental worry. Existential angst surfaces the moment you open the door and turn on the light. Now suddenly it looks just like the mysterious cavern it was when you where a child. At the end of the tunnel stands an enormous puzzle composed of bottles ranged on dusty racks. The number of bottles is irrelevant—when to comes to wine, a "vast choice" is quickly reached, and three bottles can be enough to plunge you into a wretched dilemma.

In the end, you do not really want to make up your mind. One of the basic pleasures of

Champagne should be drunk cool but not icy, from a flute or even a wine glass (*right*), but never from a coupe, which allows the aromas to dissipate. Like white wines, champagne cannot express all its subtlety if the temperature drops to 5° C (40°). Another four or five degrees centigrade (i.e., to 48° to 49° F) suit it perfectly. The most wine-like of champagnes, to be drunk with a meal (accompanying fish or poultry), should be served at 11° C (51° F). The best way to cool a bottle of champagne quickly is still to plunge it in a bucket of cold water for a few minutes (*above*). Depending on the desired serving temperature, ice may or may not be added to the bucket. Finally, contrary to entrenched popular belief, champagne—at least the great champagnes—profit a great deal from being decanted a few minutes prior to drinking, allowing their bouquet to be deployed more fully with no perceptible loss of fizz.

wine is here, as you let your gaze wonder from one label to the next in the satisfaction —tinged with a suggestion of complacency— of contemplating these venerable bottles (considered a hundred times, but never opened), of ferreting out new finds from bottles discovered during a chance trip or encounter, of those surprising wines which can be every bit as seductive—on a good night and with good guests—as a truly great vintage.

The climb back up the steps is made all the swifter by the sudden recollection that you promised not to spend too long down there. Soon other delights will follow, all intimately intertwined with a vague anxiety—did you make the right choice? The ritual that wine lovers like to observe before drinking their first mouthful of a wine is of course fully justified by the demands of good taste and manners. But most of all, it helps to prolong the pleasure.

When the conversation turns to wine, someone is always drawn in. It is a subject which stimulates conversation as much as tastebuds. As the bottle is being opened, the wine's qualities will already be under discussion. As a drop is poured into a glass—just to check that the wine is not corked—conversation will focus on the specific family of wines, on other vintages from the same estate, just as people ruminate on the minor shortcomings and major qualities of members of a large dynasty. As the wine is decanted into a carafe, conversation may shift to the neighbor's estates, as the relative merits of "Château X" and "Clos Y" are compared. Multiply a reasonable number of vintages by the number of estates in a famous wine-growing area, and you will have a fairly accurate notion of the potential number of topics of conversation open to wine lovers waiting for dinner to be served.

The great wine is now in your glass, ready to be tasted. One person and one person alone must now rise to the wine—the drinker. You must want to drink it, you must have a pretty good idea what to expect (but not *too* good), you must be prepared, and you must share it with others who can also savor the moment. Then come the memories—connoisseurs of great wines have their heads full of them.

"I mopped up the best of the paternal cellar, delicately, glass by glass... My mother re-corked the open bottle, reading the finest French vintages on my cheeks. Lucky are the children who do not bloat their stomachs with reddened water during meals! Shrewd are the parents who proffer their offspring a drop of pure wine—'pure' in the noblest sense of the term—and instruct them: Between meals, you have the pump, the faucet, the spring, the filter. Water is for thirst. Wine, depending on its quality and origin, is a necessary tonic, a luxury, an honor to cuisine." Colette, *Prisons et Paradis*. *Following page*: Two great wines for these lucky children who have now grown up—Château Laville Haut-Brion and Château Haut-Brion, both top-ranked Graves.

this wine should be se
CHÂTEAU
LE HAUT BRION
ATION GRAVES CONTRÔLÉE
Grand Cru classé
1959
SOCIÉTÉ CIVILE DES DOMAINES WOLTNER
PROPRIÉTAIRE
BORDEAUX
FRANCE
MIS EN BOUTEILLE AU CHÂTEAU
LAVILLE
CHATEAU HAU

A
Connoisseur's
Guide

THE WORLD OF WINE

This guide was produced with the help of the editorial team of *La Revue du Vin de France*, and the author would particularly like to thank Mathilde Hulot and Pascale Cassagne for their help. This is a brief presentation of the main wine-growing regions in the world with (in certain cases), a short list of producers offering wines that provide an excellent illustration of the local soil and climate, as well as being notable either for outstanding quality or for affordability. The selection is in no way exhaustive—other estates and firms not mentioned here offer very fine wines in every country and region. The French section is based on the *Classement des Vins et Domaines* (Paris: Éditions de La Revue du Vin de France), a publication issued every year by the author of this book and Michel Bettane. The German choices, meanwhile, correspond to the estates recommended most highly by our colleagues Joël Payne and Armin Diel in their excellent *WeinGuide Deutschland* (Heyne). For all other countries, the selection is based on the author's own travels and tastings.

FRANCE

Alsace
Anyone who has ever been to an Alsatian restaurant or a choucroute party is probably familiar with fine, slender Rieslings, smooth Silvaners or refreshing Pinots. And this, alas, often represents the consumer's sole recollection of the wine of Alsace. Yet few other regions of France display such variety and above all grandeur when it comes to white wines. Whether both dry or sweet (the latter resulting from late harvests or grapes with "noble rot"), the best Alsatian wines are made from Riesling, Pinot Gris or Gewürztraminer grapes, and possess the fullness and aromatic complexity of the greatest of all whites, such as for instance the finest Chardonnays. Alsace's vineyards stretch from Strasbourg to Mulhouse, along a narrow band of slopes formed essentially by the foothills of the Vosges Mountains. The mountains block masses of air in the valleys, creating a relatively dry microclimate which reinforces the effect of the continental sun during summer and fall. White grapes ripen better here than anywhere else in France, while retaining their specific fruitiness thanks to the cool hills. The wines, classified under the general banner of "Alsace" or "Alsace Grand Cru" (for fifty selected vineyards) are generally made from a single variety of grape. Silvaner gives a fresh, delicate wine, while Pinot Blanc produces the best standard wine of reliable quality from one year to the next. The two Muscats yield light, fruity wines which, in theory, should taste of the grape-berry itself. Riesling is undoubtedly the greatest Alsatian variety and, along with Chardonnay, one of the two finest varieties of white grape in the world. From good vineyards in Alsace, it displays a subtlety of taste and finesse of flavor that remain long in the mouth, making it the best wine to accompany the most refined fish dishes. This is the case when Riesling is dry, that is, because like Pinot Gris (also called Tokay in Alsace), Riesling grapes may also be picked late or allowed to acquire "noble rot," which then yield profound, rich, wines high in sugar and of great aromatic complexity—making them perfect companions to foie gras.
Some leading producers: Domaine Marcel Deiss (Bergheim), Domaine René Muré (Rouffach), Domaine Ostertag (Epfig), Cave de Pfaffenheim (Pfaffenheim), Trimbach (Ribeauvillé), Domaine Weinbach (Kaysersberg), Domaine Zind-Humbrecht (Turckheim).

Champagne
France's largest appellation covers over 30,000 hectares (72,000 acres), mostly in the administrative *départements* of the Marne, Aube and Aisne, all three at the northern limit of the possibility of ripening for grapes. With great audacity and skill, Champagne winemakers transformed an initial weakness into a strength by developing techniques that not only flatter the finesse of their grapes but also render acceptable their acidity, caused by difficulties in ripening perfectly year after year. The bubbles that form in the bottle balance this acidity and develop the mineral flavor of the grapes, which they owe to the chalky soil in which the vines grow.
Three types of firm make up the modern champagne market. Traditional traders (*négociants*) have their own vineyards of greater or lesser size but also buy grapes from a wide variety of other growers, which allows them to create complex blends, which are all the more necessary when large volumes are required. Winemaking cooperatives, meanwhile, are slowly developing their own commercial brands. Finally, estate bottlers (*vignerons récoltants*) sell wine made solely from their own vineyards. Their blends are less complex than those offered by the larger firms, but at its best the wine offers an individual cachet that is hard to beat. Producers and growers rely on particularly subtle differences in soil and climate: the Marne Valley around Épernay and Ay produces champagnes of profound, seductive balance, while Montagne de Reims (Ambonnay and Bouzy) is famous for its full-bodied champagnes with character, Côte des Blancs is known for the finesse and sparkle of it wines, and finally Aube produces reliable, robust champagnes.
Some leading producers: Billecart-Salmon (Mareuil sur Ay) Bollinger (Ay), Krug (Reims), Moët & Chandon (Avize), Roederer (Reims), Jacques Selosse (Avize), Veuve Clicquot Ponsardin (Reims), Charles Heidsieck (Reims), François Secondé (Sillery) Gatinois (Ay), Jean Vesselle (Bouzy).

Jura
The Jura region produces highly original red and rosé wines from local varieties of grape, Poulsard and Trousseau. Although lacking distinctive color, these wines are rich in tannin and have a pronounced animal flavor. The area's main great wine, however, is white and sometimes takes the "voile"—that is, a film of local yeast forms a beneficial veil in the cask, protecting the wine from oxidizing as it ages for six long years, slowly developing its flavor. Without the veil, this long aging would yield vinegar, but here it produces *vin jaune*, or yellow wine, with an inimitable flavor of nuts and mushrooms. The casks in which *vin jaune* is aged are re-used in order to lend a hint of this prestigious flavor to other, simpler white wines.
Some leading producers: Domaine Jean Macle (Château Chalon), Domaine Jacques Puffeney (Montigny les Arsures), Domaine Rolet (Arbois).

Savoy
Savoy offers many light, delicious white wines with a slightly fizzy quality, as well a very good reds made from Mondeuse grapes.
A leading producer: Domaine Raymond Quénard (Chignin).

Burgundy
No other wine can attain such quasi-sublime dimensions, just as no other wine can often seem so slight and insubstantial—therein lies the paradox of Burgundy. It produces the most refined and the most rustic of wines within a fairly limited geographical zone that extends from a few rolling slopes in the Yonne to a long east-facing bluff that runs from Dijon down to the Beaujolais hills. The finest wines are the produce of a wine-growing region steeped in history, starting with its vines of Pinot Noir and Chardonnay grapes, heirs to a long process of natural selection and perfect adaptation to soil and climate. Great Burgundies open up a little faster than wines from Bordeaux, which usually means they are best drunk at between five and twelve years for reds and three to ten years for whites. But they can also age admirably, retaining their silky texture and fruity fullness for thirty years or more without becoming parched by tannins.
This diversity of types of wine derives from

an unprecedented human and geographical jigsaw puzzle, recognized and preserved by legislation. A clear hierarchy of appellations nevertheless makes it possible to navigate through the maze of different villages and age-old names. The best *communes* enjoy the right to their own appellation, or to one that groups several neighboring *communes*. The name of a particular, precisely limited vineyard may also be added—for example Pommard, Pommard la Vache, and Pommard Rugiens. The best of these are awarded the prestigious title of *premier cru*. The truly finest vines in Burgundy are called *grand cru* and have their own appellation, no longer including the name of the *commune*, such as Bonnes-Mares or Richebourg.

In the Yonne, whites are famous for their finesse and responsiveness, as best expressed by the finest vineyards of Chablis. From Dijon to Chagny, in the *département* of Côte-d'Or, numerous villages make red and white wines of an aromatic nobility unmatched in France. Reds from Côte de Nuit tend to be more robust than those from Côte de Beaune, and may even tend towards violence in their youth; in both districts, little known villages just a stone's throw from those more famous sometimes yield fabulous treasures to adventurous wine lovers at a modest price. Finally, Côte Chalonnaise produces extremely pleasant whites and reds, slightly less complex than Côte-d'Or but at reasonable prices. The Mâcon area, on the edge of Beaujolais, specializes in magnificent whites that are still too little known. Beaujolais is where the kingdom of the Gamay grape begins—in the most brilliant fahion, as this is where the grape's most full-bodied wines are made (Saint-Amour, Juliénas, Moulin à Vent, Chenas and Fleurie).

Some leading producers: **Chablis:** Domaine René et Vincent Dauvissat, Domaine Raveneau, La Chablisienne. **Côte de Nuits:** Domaine Jean Trapet (Gevrey Chambertin), Domaine Georges Roumier (Chambolle Musigny), Domaine Perrot-Minot (Morey Saint Denis), Domaine Faiveley (Nuits Saint Georges), Domaine Dugat-Py (Gevrey Chambertin), Domaine Denis Mortet (Gevrey Chambertin), Domaine Bruno Clair (Marasannay la Côte), Domaine Comtes de Vogüé (Chambolle Musigny), Domaine Henry Gouges (Nuits Saint Georges), Domaine de la Romanée Conti (Vosne Romanée), Domaine Jean Grivot (Vosne Romanée), Domaine Méo-Camuzet (Vosne Romanée). **Côte de Beaune:** Domaine Ramonet (Chassagne Montrachet), Domaine Bonneau du Martray (Pernand Vergelesses), Domaine Tollot-Beaut (Chorey lès Beaune), Domaine Coche-Dury (Meursault), Domaine des Comtes Lafond (Meursault), Jean-Marc Boillot (Pommard), Domaine du Comte Armand (Pommard), Domaine de Montille (Volnay), Domaine Leflaive (Puligny Montachet), Olivier Leflaive (Puligny Montrachet), Etienne Sauzet (Puligny

Montrachet), Domaine Simon Bize (Savigny lès Baune), Domaine Marquis d'Angerville (Meursault). **Côte Chalonnaise:** Domaine René Bourgeon (Givry), Domaine Joblot (Givry). **Mâconnais:** Domaine de La Bongran (Clessé), Domaine Pierre-Marie Chermette (Saint Vérand), Georges Duboeuf (Romanèche Thorins), Henry Fessy (Saint Jean d'Ardières), Hubert Lapierre (La Chapelle de Guinchay), Jean Foillard (Villé Morgon), Château des Jacques (Romanèche Thorins). **All Burgundies:** Antonin Rodot (Mercurey), Verget (Sologny), Domaine d'Auvenay (Meursault), Bouchard Père et Fils (Beaune), Louis Jadot (Beaune), Dominique Laurent (Nuits Saint Georges), Domaine Leroy (Auxey Duresses), Domaine Jacques Prieur (Meursault).

Rhône Valley

This is a vast wine-growing region, beginning on the steep slopes of Côte Rôtie less than twenty miles south of Lyon and spreading over hills, plateaux and plains as far as Avignon, over one hundred miles downstream. Because it stretches from an austere and sometimes harsh valley all the way to sunny Provence, the area is schematically—but not unreasonably—divided into two distinct regions: the north, from Vienne to Valence, and the south, from Bollène to Avignon. The former favors a single variety of grape (Syrah for reds, Viognier or Marsanne for whites), while the latter takes a mischievous pleasure in combining and blending quite different varieties, although Grenache is the dominant red.

The northern region is planted essentially on the granite slopes rising above the right and left banks of the Rhône River, sometimes spilling onto the plateaux of the Massif Central (Côte Rôtie, Condrieu, Saint-Joseph) or the occasional alluvial plain (Crozes-Hermitage). In contrast, the south exploits a much more varied landscape, ranging from hills to alluvial plans, and from plateaux to terraces. The geology of the area is extremely varied, so that the land around Châteauneuf-du-Pape includes not only the famous rounded pebbles seen on every postcard of the area, but also limestone and sandy soils. Other major districts in the south include Gigondas, Vacqueyras, Lirac, and Tavel, plus many worthy village vineyards included in the Côte-du-Rhône-Villages appellation.

Over and above their differences, one characteristic unites all these wines: their extreme drinkability. The ideal profile of the finest Rhône wines translates into reds bursting with health, color, and richly endowed fruit, and whites that are fleshy and aromatic.

Some leading producers: **All Rhône wines:** Étienne Guigal (Ampuis), Jabolet-Aîné (Tain l'Hermitage), M. Chapoutier (Tain l'Hermitage), Domaine Tardieu Laurent (Lauris). **Condrieu:** Domaine Georges Vernay. **Crozes-Hermitage:** Alain Graillot.

Cornas: Domaine Colombo. **Hermitage:** Domaine Jean-Louis Chave (Mauve), Domaine Marc Sorel (Tain l'Hermitage), Cave de Tain (Tain l'Hermitage). **Côtes du Rhône-Villages:** Domaine Marcel Richaud (Cairanne), Domaine de l'Oratoire Saint-Martin (Cairanne). **Châteauneuf-du-Pape:** Château de Beaucastel (Courthezon), Château La Nerthe (Châteauneuf-du-Pape), Château Rayas (Châteauneuf-du-Pape). **Gigondas:** Domaine Les Goubert. **Lirac:** Domaine de la Mordorée (Tavel).

Languedoc-Roussillon

The vineyards of Languedoc and Roussillon have undergone an extraordinary renaissance in quality in the past quarter century. This is undoubtedly the region that holds the greatest potential for new discoveries. The *départements* of Gard and Hérault jointly make up the appellation Coteaux du Languedoc, which includes many fine wines such as Pic-Saint-Loup, Montpeyroux, Saint Chinian and Faugères (reds), La Clappe (red and white), and Picpoul de Pinet (white). In the *département* of Aude, the straightforward, fleshy wines of Minervois are attractive, as are the warmer wines of Fitou and Corbières. In Roussillon, alongside reds and whites sold under the appellation Côtes du Roussillon and the small Collioure vintage (which yields balanced, rather fine reds), interest lies above all in the naturally sweet whites of Banyuls, Maury and Rivesaltes; a certain percentage of their residual sugar is retained by halting fermentation through the addition of pure alcohol, the same method used to make port.

Some leading producers: **Languedoc:** Mas Jullien (Jonquières), Domaine d'Aupillac (Montpeyroux), Prieuré Saint-Jean de Bébian (Pézenas), Mas Bruguières (Valflaunes), Fortant de France (Sète), Mas de Daumas Gassac (Aniane). **Roussillon:** Domaine des Chênes (Vingrau), Domaine Gauby (Calce), Domaine Cazes Frères (Rivesaltes). **Banyuls:** L'Étoile, Domaine du Mas Blanc, Cellier des Templiers, Vial-Magnères.

Provence and Corsica

With the exception of Bandol, where the profound originality of soil, climate and variety have catapulted local wines into the tiny club of great French reds, the reputation of Provence and Corsica rests mainly on their rosé wines. In the past two or three decades, however, they have benefited from the dynamism, talent, enthusiasm and investment of men and women with the determination to make great wine.

Hence it is now possible to find numerous reds, rosés and whites that are charming and elegant, often displaying a style linked more to the winemaker than to a particular soil or climate. Among the appellations worth noting are Côtes de Provence, Palette and Cassis for finely aromatic whites, Bandol for the finest reds in Provence, and the Corsican wines of Patrimonio, Cap Corse, Porto-Vecchio, Ajaccio, and Calvi, for reds, rosés and whites, and especially their delicious Muscats.

Some leading producers: **Les Baux de Provence:** Domaine de Trévallon (Saint Étienne du Grès). **Bandol:** Château Pradeau (Saint Cyr sur Mer), Château Vannières (La Cadière d'Azur). **Côtes de Provence:** Château Réal Martin (Le Val). **Palette:** Château Simone (Meyreuil). **Corse Patrimonio:** Domaine Antoine Arena (Patrimonio).

Southwest

Although the "black wine" of Cahors was more famous than claret in the Middle Ages, Bordeaux's easy access and maritime power subsequently ensued its rise to prominence. Not far from the Bordeaux region, the Bergerac vineyards built their reputation in the nineteenth and early twentieth century on sweet wines, especially those from Monbazillac. Although less powerful than Sauternes, they are worth rediscovering today, for they possess true depth and their own full-blossomed style. Cahors offers, on the one hand, rounded, supple, easy to drink wines of no ambition other than to rival minor Bordeaux wines, and on the other, more ambitious vintages that are simultaneously vigorous and elegant. Further south, at the foot of the Pyrenees, the vineyards of Jurançon and Madiran are returning to their former glory. Sweet Jurançon wines are like no other: rich, sappy, thoroughbred and endowed with highly original vivacity. Madiran, finally, provides a rare example of a traditional vineyard that has been brilliantly transformed under several producers to yield wines of power and refinement.

Some leading producers: **Bergerac**: Château Tour des Gendres (Ribagnac). **Cahors:** Château du Cèdre (Vire sur Lot), Château Gautoul (Puy l'Évêque), **Gaillac:** Domaine Robert Plageoles (Cahuzac sur Vère). **Jurançon:** Clos Uroulat (Monein). **Madiran:** Château Montus (Maumusson), Château Bouscassé (Maumusson).

Bordeaux

The *département* of Gironde produces over six million hectoliters of wine per year, making it, along with the Hérault and the Aude, the most prolific in France. It is clear, therefore, that Bordeaux is not always synonymous with great wines or expensive vintages. There is nevertheless one characteristic shared by all Bordeaux wines, from the humblest to the most famous: they are never heavy, and can be drunk easily and on all occasions. Even the most "opulent" of them—Pomerol or, in a completely different genre, Sauternes—possess that welcome freshness that is so often lacking in many other wines, famous or not.

Clearly, this quality alone is hardly enough to satisfy demanding connoisseurs. Bordeaux's

international prestige is founded first of all on the impressive palette of great wines the region has to offer: the eminently aristocratic distinction of the best Médocs, the sappy depth of Saint-Émilions and Pomerols, the great harmony of both reds and whites from Graves, the mature magnificence of sweet Sauternes and Barsacs. Although Graves and Entre-deux-Mers on the opposite bank of the Garonne produce many dry white wines, and although Sauternes makes the most famous sweet white wine in the world, Bordeaux remains above all known for its reds. Two major styles co-exist: wines from the right bank of the Garonne (which flows into the Gironde), and those from the left bank. On the right bank, heading upstream, are the vineyards of prestigious Médocs (Margaux, Saint-Julien, Pauillac, Saint-Estèphe, etc.), Pessac-Léognan and Graves. These wines are often characterized by the straightforward power of the Cabernet Sauvignon grape. On the left bank, not far from Libourne, come the vineyards of Pomerol and Saint-Émilion, with wines displaying the roundness and generosity of Merlot grapes.

The finest Bordeaux vineyards have been officially classified. The principal classification, conducted for the 1855 Universal Exposition in Paris and still unchanged today (with one exception) in fact applies only to Médoc and Château Haut-Brion in Graves on the one hand, and to Sauternes on the other. The sole modification in this ranking dates from 1973, when Château Mouton-Rothschild was promoted to *premier cru.*

Some leading producers: **Bordeaux:** Château Bonnet (Grezillac). **Haut-Médoc:** Château Sociando-Mallet (Saint Seurin de Cadourne). **Margaux:** Château Margaux, Château Palmer, Château Rauzan-Ségla. **Moulis:** Château Poujeaux. **Saint-Julien:** Château Branaire, Château Ducru-Beaucaillou, Château Gruand-Larose, Château Léoville-Barton, Château Léoville-Las Cases, Château Léoville-Poyferré, Château Saint-Pierre, Château Talbot. **Pauillac:** Château Lafite-Rothschild, Château Pichon-Longueville, Château Pichon-Longueville Comtesse de Lalande, Château Pontent-Canet. **Saint-Estèphe:** Château Cos d'Estournel, Château Haut-Marbuzet, Château Lafond-Rochet, Château Phélan-Ségur, Château Montrose. **Pessac-Léognan:** Domaine de Chevalier, Château Haut-Brion, Château Haut-Bailly, Château La Mission Haut-Brion, Château Pape-Clément, Château Smith Haut-Lafitte. **Graves:** Château de Chantegrive (Podensac), Clos Floridène (Beguey). **Canon-Fronsac:** Château Grand-Renouil. **Pomerol:** Château Clinet (Saint Germain du Puch), Château Gazin (Pomerol), Château L'Évangile (Pomerol), Château Lafleur (Rouillac), Château Le Bon Pasteur (Pomerol), Château Pétrus (Pomerol), Vieux Château Certan (Pomerol). **Saint-Émilion:** Château Angélus, Château Ausone, Château Beauséjour, Château Canon La Gaffelière, Château Cheval-Blanc, Château

Grand Mayne, Château Troplong-Mondot, Château Larcis-Ducasse. **Sauternes:** Château Gilette (Preignac), Château Guiraud (Sauternes), Château Lafaurie-Peyraguey (Bommes), Château Clos Haut-Peyraguey (Bommes) Château Suduiraut (Preignac), Château d'Yquem (Sauternes), Château Climens (Barsac), Château Doisy-Daëne (Barsac).

The Loire Valley

The Loire Valley is capable of producing all types of wine, from the most concentrated sweet wines to bone-dry ones, from young wines to age-old vintages, from fruity, grapey flavors to the mineral taste of the soil. Trying to organize all this according to locality, variety and appellation has made the Loire wine-growing region one of the most complex in France. The best way to make sense of it is to follow the river upstream from its mouth. Starting in the Nantes region, Muscadet produces dry, light white wines that often have a hint of sparkle; next, Anjou's rich agricultural heritage yields a full range of wines (whites, reds, rosés, dry, "medium-dry", sweet) such as the deliciously scented Coteaux de l'Aubance, Coteaux du Layon, Bonnezeaux and Quarts de Chaume—and even effervescent wines; Saumur is notable for its sparkling wines and especially for a remarkable red from Saumur-Champigny; Touraine boasts the supple, fruity red wines made from Cabernet Franc grapes in Chinon, Bourgueil, and Saint-Nicolas-de-Bourgueil (which can attain great heights during good years), and fine, silky wines from Montlouis and Vouvray, able to age for several decades. Finally, the magnificent clayey-limestone slopes of Sancerre, Morogue and Pouilly-sur-Loire grow a Sauvignon grape that performs great feats of finesse when harvested at the peak of maturity.

Some leading producers: **Muscadet:** Domaine de l'Écu (Le Landreau). **Anjou:** Château de Fesles (Thouarcé), Château Pierre Bize (Beaulieu sur Layon), Domaine Joe Pithon (Saint Lambert du Lattray), Coulée de Serrant (Savennières). **Saumur:** Clos Rougeard (Chacé), Château de Villeneuve (Sousay Champigny). **Touraine:** Domaine Philippe Alliet (Cravant les Coteaux), Domaine Charles Joguet (Sazilly), Domaine Henry Marionnet (Soings), Domaine Huet (Vouvray), Clos Baudoin (Vouvray), Domaine Yannick Amirault (Bourgueil). **Hauts-de-Loire**: Domaine Dagueneau (Saint Andelain), Château du Nozet (Pouilly sur Loire), Domaine Lucien Crochet (Bué), Domaine Alphonse Mellot (Sancerre).

OTHER EUROPEAN COUNTRIES

Italy

Italy is the world's leading wine producer, with an average annual output of sixty million hectoliters, or one-fifth of the global total. Italy is also the largest exporter of wine

WINE IN EUROPE

(one quarter of its national output). Vines grow in a tremendous variety of landscapes. Accustomed to producing in great volume for its own consumers and for pizzerias all over the world, it was only very recently, in the 1960s, that the country acquired the notion of making fine wines.

Tuscany. This multi-crop region in north-central Italy (Florence, Pisa, Siena) essentially produces red wines made primarily from Sangiovese grapes, combined with Cabernet, Merlot, and others. It is the cradle of Chianti, Brunello di Montalcino, and the *vino nobile* of Montepulciano further inland. Chianti forged its astonishing reputation in the thirteenth century, and its popularity has led to frequent illicit use of the name and to administrative enlargement of the zone, leading to great disparities in quality. The finest vineyards are located around Siena. Further south, Brunello di Montalcino is a sea of vines in the midst of arid plains, which benefits from Mediterranean breezes. The region is planted with Brunello (a synonym for Sangiovese) and, on an experimental basis, Cabernet grapes. Wines with a reputation for fine aging surfaced from the cellars of Biondi-Santi in the 1960s and saw their prices rocket, whereupon everyone decided to plant vines and the area grew from less than 100 hectares (240 acres) in 1968 (when the appellation zone, *Denominazione di Origine Controllata*, or DOC, was established) to over 900. Tuscany is also home to the fine, elegant red known as *vino nobile* from Montepulciano, as well as Rosso di Montepulciano, Ornellaia (made from Cabernet grapes), Bolgheri (also Cabernet), Masseto (Merlot) and *vino santo*.

Some leading producers: Villa Antinori (Florence), Isole e Olana (Florence) Marchesi di Frescobaldi (Florence) Castello di Ama (Lecchi), Castello di Volpaia (Volpaia), Castello di Fonterutoli (Fonterutoli), Castello di Sassicaia (Belgheri), Avignonesi (Montepulciano).

Piedmont. Situated at the foot of the Alps in northwestern Italy, Piedmont boasts the greatest number of DOC appellations and undoubtedly possesses the greatest potential in terms of the country's fine red wines. Italy's most famous vineyards flank the Alba River, namely Barolo (1,300 hectares) and Barbaresco (500 hectares). Both are made from the Nebbiolo grape, a variety that yields vigorous, profound wines; Barolo takes longer to age whereas Barbaresco is finer and more supple. Piedmont also produces Dolcetto, a fruity red made from grapes of the same name, and Barbera, a firm, dense red. Finally, the vineyards at Asti make the famous *spumante*, a sparkling wine of uneven quality.

Some leading producers: Gaja (Barbaresco), Domenico Cerico d'Altare (La Morra), Conteno (Monforte d'Alba), Bruno Rocca (Barbaresco), Sandrone (Barolo), Roverto Verzio (La Morra).

The Veneto. This northeastern region of Italy is known for Valpolicella, a ruby-colored, fruity, aromatic red that is rich yet delicate.

Friuli. In this region close to the Austrian and Slovenian borders, reds and above all whites are made in large quantities (over one million hectoliters) from Merlot, Cabernet, Pinot Noir, Refosco, Ribolla Nera (for the reds) and Pinot Gris, Riesling, Tocai Friulano, Traminer and others (for the whites). The wines are fresh, straightforward and simple, and are intended to be drunk fairly young.

Sicily and Sardinia. These two Italian islands are currently undergoing a winemaking transformation. Sicily alone accounts for ten million hectoliters of wine (a quarter of the country's exports), of which only 180,000 hectoliters are DOC quality. Worth noting are Marsala (which recalls Portuguese Madeira), Muscato di Pantelleria, and Malvasia delle Lipari, two sweet wines from small island lying to the south an north respectively of the larger island.

Spain

Spain holds the record for surface-area of vineyards with 1.2 million hectares (2.9 million acres) in 1996. In terms of volume of wine, however, it comes well behind Italy and France. The country has widely varying landscapes and soils that produce all kinds of wine, and was first planted with vines in 1100 BC, when the Phoenicians founded Cadiz. The Greeks, Carthaginians and Romans then extended their cultivation throughout the land. Nowadays, Spain produces high-volume wines in La Mancha and Castilla La Nueva, as well as highly reputed or original wines in places such as Rioja, Rivera del Duero, Jerez, and Malaga. Spain is also known for its interesting local varieties and above all for its long aging in oak.

Rioja. The region may be divided into three zones: Rioja Alta, whose climate would be similar to Bordeaux if it were not for late frosts and a hot wind called the *solano*, and which therefore produces the finest wines, Rioja Alavesa and Rioja Baja, which make more more ordinary wines. Winemaking is done in long-established *bodegas* (Marquès de Riscal, Marquès de Murieta, Cune, etc.) which have developed a long tradition of blending grapes from many small growers.
Some leading producers: Marquès de Cacerès (Cenicero), Contino (Laserna), Cune (Haro), El Coto (Oyon).

Ribera del Duero ("Bank of the Douro") is Spain's up-and-coming region. Located in Castilla-Leon, less than 120 miles from Madrid and at an altitude of some 2,500 feet, the area became known in the mid nineteenth century with the founding of the *bodega* Pago de la Vega Santa Sicilia y Carrascul, later simply called Vega Sicilia. Bordeaux grapes were used to make a *tinto fino* that became wildly popular. In the late 1970s, Pesquera was launched, and in 1982 the district was granted appellation status. Ever since, the region's velvety, fresh, extremely fruity wines have consistently seduced wine-lovers.
Some leading producers: Pesquera (Arenda del Duero), Condado de Haza (Arenda del Duero), Arzuaga (Arenda del Duero), Akion (Arenda del Duero), Vega Sicilia (Valbuena del Duero).

Catalonia. The region possesses two favorites: Penedes (a region dynamized by a certain Miquel Torrès as early as 1961) and Cava (a Spanish-style sparkling wine).
A leading producer: Torrès (Villafranca).
Among more unusual wines, two are leaders in the field. **Sherry** (11,600 hectares) is made around Jerez de la Frontera, south of Seville, from the Palomino grape (90%), in three styles: fino (light, hint of green apple), manzanilla (saline, bitter), and oloroso (full-bodied, nutty). **Malaga** from Andalusia (1,000 hectares) is made with Pedro Ximenez and Airén grapes, enriched with *arrope* (the juice of boiled grapes) and aged by the *solera* method.
Some leading sherry producers: Barbadillo (San-Lucar de Barrameda), Pedro Domecq (Jerez de la Frontera), Lustau (Jerez de la Frontera), Osborne (Puerto), Valdespino (Jerez de la Frontera).

Portugal
Portugal makes three types of wine—port, madeira, and standard wine (red, white and rosé).
Port. Port wines come from the vineyards flanking the Douro River to the east of the city of Porto. The region became the first appellation in the world when the Marquis de Pombal decreed in 1756 that the zone should extend some sixty miles downstream from Regua on the Spanish border, where steep slopes plunge down to the Douro. Port was born of shipping requirements: the English added brandy to wine to help it withstand the trip, and the resulting drink retained some additional sweetness. The grapes used are the Touriga Nacional, Tinta Roriz and Tinta Barroca, with some Tintas (or Sosão) for color. White port, meanwhile, is made from Vedelho, Malvasia, Rabigato and Esgana Cao. These wines, sometimes of ordinary quality, can also attain heights that remain unknown—alas—to most consumers. The major firms produce vintage port (bottled rapidly and only in the best years) and tawny port (aged in casks) of an incomparable finesse and complexity.
Some leading producers: Fonseca, Graham, Quinta do Noval, Taylor, Warre's, Barros, Ramos Pinto.

Madeira. In 1418, the Portuguese prince Henry the Navigator dispatched Juan Gonçalves Zarco to conquer the island of Madeira, which was so heavily wooded that no one had been able to penetrate it (Madeira means "wood"). Some 35 miles long and 9 miles wide, the island lies 400 miles off the Moroccan coast, some 500 miles from Lisbon. In 1753, the first casks of madeira wine were topped up with a little brandy to enable them to reach the East Indies unspoiled. Madeira wine attained the height of its popularity in the eighteenth and nineteenth centuries. Today the island's 1,600 hectares (3,800 acres) of vineyards yield 30,000 hectoliters of madeira for export.
Most of the wine produced and sold throughout Portugal is standard white, red and rosé (Mateus and Lancers are among the best-sellers worldwide). The 1988 output reached 8 million hectoliters. There are thirteen official appellations (Denominação de Origem Controlada, DOC), including Vinho Verde, a large region to the north and east of Porto which produces a "green" wine—in fact, a spritzy white—which ows its name primarily to the extreme greenness of the landscape. The Douro (around Porto) makes appealing reds, as does the Dão to the south. To the east of the Dão, Bairrada is the realm of the aromatic Baga grape for red wines, although the area also makes white and sparkling wines. Finally, it is worth mentioning Alentejo, a large southeastern region bordering Spain, which produces fruity, tannic reds of highly attractive potential.

Switzerland
Swiss vineyards cover some 15,000 hectares (36,000 acres), divided unequally between the French-speaking part (11,000 hectares), the German-speaking part (3,000 hectares) and the Italian-speaking part (1,000 hectares). Only a tiny percentage of domestic production is exported (10,000 hectoliters out of 1.3 million in 1996). Vines tend to line the shores of lakes, making Swiss vineyards some of the most picturesque in the world. The French-speaking zone includes the cantons of the Valais, Vaud and Geneva. The Valais, which follows the course of the upper Rhône before it flows into Lake Geneva, grows Fendant (the local name for Chasselas), which yields a light, fresh wine of the same name, and Johannisberger (or Silvaner), which is drunk with asparagus. It also produces Dôle, a wine created in the 1850s by pressing and fermenting together Pinot Noir and Gamay. In addition to Riesling, other Swiss varieties include Amigne, Humagne, Arvine (three local grapes) and Malvasia (Pinot Gris), which makes some interesting late-picked wines. The canton of Vaud, meanwhile, produces mostly white wines (80%) primarily from Chasselas but also Silvaner, Pinot Gris, Müller-Thürgau, Chardonnay and Muscat. Pinot Noir and Gamay are used for reds. Geneva's vineyards form a ring around the city, and yield dry, light rather spritzy wines. In the German-speaking region to the northeast of the country, seventeen cantons (notably Zurich) make both reds (from Pinot Noir, known locally as Blauburgunder) and whites (from Riesling-Silvaner, known as Müller-Thürgau).

Greece
Mentioned in *The Iliad* and *The Odyssey*, Greek wine and vineyards boast one of the oldest documented histories. Legislation passed in 1976 recognized twenty-eight appellations over a total of 132,000 hectares (320,00 acres). Among the most important and best known are Peloponnesus (which produces 25% of the country's 4.1 million hectoliters) and Attica (to the south of Athens, where retsina reigns, representing 15% of output). Central and western Macedonia make interesting reds, notably Carras (created by a family of Greek ship owners) and Naoussa, based on the local Xynomavro grape. Then come the countless islands, each more beautiful than the last, but producing wines of uneven quality: the Aegean islands (Samos, Lemnos and Lesbos), the Cyclades (Santorini with its volcanic soil and Paros), the Ionian islands (Corfu, Zante, Keffalina and Levkas), and Crete, which boasts four appellations: Archanes, Peza (both white) and Sitia and Dafnes (both red).

Germany
German vineyards are among the most northerly in the world. They are located in the southwestern part of the country, with the exception of Saale-Unstrut and Saxony, in the southern part of former East Germany. In these less propitious climates, vines are cultivated primarily along river banks (Rhine, Main, Nahe, Mosel and its tributaries, the Saar and Ruwer), where the cold is mitigated and the mists help to ward off early

frosts. The history of German wine-growing dates back to the early Christian era, and owes its development to monastic activities after the feudal wars. Today's 105,000 hectares (240,000 acres) produce an annual average of 10 million hectoliters (8.3 million in 1996) of largely white wine (87%). The vineyards are divided into eleven *Qualitätswein* regions (known as *Angaugebiete*), broken down into thirty-four districts (*Bereiche*), 152 groups of several communes (*Grosslagen*), and 2,600 individual vineyards (*Einzellagen*).

The Mosel/Saar/Ruwer and the Rheingau regions produce the most extraordinary dry and especially sweet white wines found in Germany or anywhere else in the world.

Mosel/Saar/Ruwer Valley. It is the slate soil of this region which lends its wines their unique character. Here some fifty *Bereiche* are planted with at least 50% Riesling grapes, a variety which in great years yields outstanding wines, such as Schwarzhofberger TBA (*Trockenbeerenauslese*, meaning a selection of noble grapes); those made by Egon Müller are some of the most expensive in the world. The Ruwer wines are lighter than those of Mosel and Saar.

Some leading producers: Fritz Haag (Braunberg) Egon Müller (Wiltingen), Jos Prüm (Bernkastel) Von Schubert (Grünhaus-Mertesdorf).

Rheingau wines can also attain unparalleled heights. Located twenty miles from Frankfurt, the vineyards overlook the Rhine on splendid south-facing slopes protected by the Taunus hills. In the unique *Bereich* of Johannisberg, some 286 different types of soils favorable to Riesling have been identified. Rheingau owes its success to excellent natural conditions allied with the dedication and financial resources of long-established estates such as Schloss Johannisberg and Schloss Reinhartshausen.

Some leading producers: Robert Weil (Kiedrich), Georg Breuer (Rüdesheim), Johannishof (Johannisberg), Jakob Kuhn (Oestrich-Winkel).

The Rheinpfalz merits attention as it is a carbon copy of Alsace (river, variety, landscape) on the German side of the border. It produces wines in large quantities from the plain (Liebfraumilch), but also, thanks to generous amounts of sunshine, boasts slope-grown wines with body and elegance.

Austria

After being abandoned at the end of the Roman empire, Austria's vineyards were replanted in 955 and long maintained by monks. Nowadays they cover 52,000 hectares (125,000 acres), uniquely in the eastern part of the country, and produce over 2 million hectoliters of wine annually. Many varieties of grape are grown, from Grüner Veltliner to Pinot Blanc via Welschriesling, Traminer, Müller-Thürgau, Blauburgender (Pinot Noir) and Blaufränkisch (Gamay), in three main regions: Lower Austria, Steiermark, and Burgenland. Lower Austria, to the north, straddles the Danube around Vienna, and is known for its spicy, lively Grüner Veltliner. Steiermark (or Styria), to the south, lies close to Italy and Slovenia and, like them, has landscape of the Alpine foothills. Southern Steiermark produces Chardonnay (known as Morillon), Sauvignon and Gelber Muskateller. But it is undoubtedly Burgenland, which belonged to Hungary before the 1920 treaty, which produces the most interesting wines. The shores of Neusiedler See, swampy and misty in the fall, give birth to Ruster-Ausbruch, one of the finest and purest of all sweet wines. Blaufränkisch, meanwhile, finds its ideal conditions to the south, in mid Burgenland, where it yields superb, tannic reds that are rich and velvety, becoming somewhat lighter further south. Finally, Vienna can claim to be the world's only true wine-producing capital city, with vineyards on hillsides within the city limits and in surrounding villages, such as Grinzing and Heiligenstadt, which each year celebrate their new wine, Heurigen.

Hungary

Hungarian vineyards may be roughly divided into three regions: the shores of Lake Balaton to the west (a major tourist attraction in a land-locked country), the vast vineyards of the great central plain stretching from the Serbian border to Eger in the north, and finally the Tokay district in the northeast. The Lake Balaton area produces mostly white wines, more or less sweet, with Keknyelü grapes producing the most interesting. Apart from Eger, the vineyards of the central plain lie on sandy (formerly swampy) land that yields reds and whites of middling ambition; although Egri Bikaver ("Bull's Blood") no longer lives up to its reputation as a great red, the quality of wines from the vineyards of Eger—especially the whites—indicates that they have real potential. Finally the Tokay vineyards—or rather, Tokaji, as the village is called—produces not only the famous sweet *aszu* Tokay but also dry and off-dry whites such as Szamorodni. Hungary has a wide range of native grape varieties. The most interesting whites include the straightforward, lively and powerful Furmint (used in Tokay), the more aromatic Hàrslevelü (Tokay and the rest of the country), and Keknyelü (Lake Balaton area). Western varieties, notably Sauvignon and Chardonnay—are also clearly gaining place in the Balaton vineyards.

Some leading producers: Disnökö (Tokay), Oremus (Tokay), Royal Tokaj Company (Tokay), Hetszölö (Tokay).

Although still little known to western consumers, the wines of **Slovakia** and the **Czech Republic** show real promise, at least as far as the whites are concerned. Most of the vineyards are located in the middle of the former Czechoslovakia, in Moravia on the Czech side, and around Bratislava on the Slovakian side.

In the nineteenth and early twentieth century, **Slovenia** was well known to traders in Bordeaux, Cognac and Porto—not for its wines, but for the quality of its oak, then considered the best in the world for making high quality casks. Today Slovenia hopes to build a reputation as a producer of fine wines. It has the resources, because it began producing western-style wines earlier than other countries of eastern Europe (apart from Bulgaria), that is to say dry, non-oxidized wines made from internationally fashionable varieties.

The vineyards of **Croatia, Bosnia** and **Montenegro** boast a very ancient heritage. Located on the Dalmatian coast and islands, they mostly benefit from a limestone subsoil suited notably to the production of white wines. The sloping vineyards (often terraced) enjoy a perfect southern exposure to the hot Mediterranean sun.

Central **Serbia**, along with hilly Slavonia and the Vojvodine region, produces good whites, often from Riesling or related grapes (Grasevina), but also from Sauvignon and Gewürztraminer (Traminac). **Macedonia**'s many vineyards produce mostly red wines. Most of these wines are drunk locally, but it is not impossible to imagine that some day these countries, under more peaceful conditions, might introduce them to a wider public. Their incomparable variety of soils, climates and grapes alone indicates a wonderful potential for high quality.

Bulgaria is a special case among countries of the former eastern bloc: in the 1950s it was the only one to plant in bulk vines that were either French (Merlot, Cabernet Sauvignon, Chardonnay) or German (Riesling, Traminer). As a country with no particular wine-making tradition, Bulgaria thus became the "obligatory" supplier to its Soviet big brother. New vineyards were planted on the fertile land stretching from the center of the country to the Black Sea coast, in the expectation of producing wines of decent quality. In the event, such hopes were largely surpassed, as the vines began to yield enormous quantities of wine representing excellent value for money.

Although **Romania**'s vineyards, like those of Bulgaria, were extensively developed in the 1960s, here a local variety was used, for Romania has a very ancient wine-growing tradition. One of its wines, Cotnari, was a highly prized dessert wine on the aristocratic tables of nineteenth-century Europe.

A continental climate and very hot summers make perfect growing conditions, and numerous vineyards are found throughout the country: in the southern Carpathians (where French and German varieties have recently been planted, including Cabernet, Merlot, Pinot Noir, Riesling, and others), Transylvania in the centre of the country, and above all in Moldavia (the home of Cotnari) and short Black Sea coastline (notably around Murflatar, known for both its reds and its sweet whites).

Finally, **Russia** and the former republics of the Soviet Union contain a great many vineyards, still mostly devoted to the production of very modest wines. However, with an output of 40 million hectoliters per year, the **C.I.S.** is the world's third-largest producer, after Italy and France. Its vineyards all lie in the countries or regions that stretch in an arc around the Black Sea: Azerbaijan, Armenia and Georgia, Ingush, Dagestan, Rostov and Stavropol (these latter four in Russia), and the Crimea and Odessa (in the Ukraine).

NORTH AMERICA

United States

California

Although many other parts of the USA produce wine (vineyards exist in 25 states), only California has shown sufficient enthusiasm to make it a major agricultural activity (roughly 15 million hectoliters per year) and above all to initiate a ruthless revolution in quality unmatched anywhere else in the world. The state's wine industry displays typically American degree of pragmatism and dynamism.

California's vineyards date back to the eighteenth century (which is not bad for wine-growing region still described as "new"!), but their true development came only a century later, at the hands of French, German and Hungarian immigrants who arrived once California became part of the US. In 1890, Californians were already producing over one million hectoliters. Wine-drinking remained nevertheless limited to certain ethnic groups, and the vineyards were hit by the nationwide prohibition laws introduced in 1918. The industry therefore had to start again almost from scratch after World War II. It did so initially by banking on wines of reliable uality and then, starting in the 1950s, by attempting to make some truly great wines, notably from French grapes such as Cabernet Sauvignon and Merlot (for reds) and Chardonnay (for whites).

In general, climatic differences between wine districts are more significant from west to east (cooler on the coast, hotter inland) than from north to south.

Mendocino County. This northern county has vineyards that are generally some distance from the ocean and set in alluvial valleys between low hills, making for hot and fairly dry summers. Anderson Valley, however, has cooler weather, thanks to morning mists, which perhaps explains the arrival of certain French firms from Champagne (Roederer Estate, for example) making high quality sparkling wines.

Some leading producers: Fetzer (Redwood), McDowell (Hopland), Roederer Estate (Berkeley).

Sonoma County. Along with Napa County, Sonoma boasts the highest number of famous wineries. Stretching from just north of San Francisco up to Mendocino, the area features vineyards running along the Pacific valleys, such as Dry Creek, Russian River, Green Valley, and Sonoma Valley. It is hard to attribute a specific style to the Sonoma wines, firstly because the region is vast, and secondly because American individualism and enterprising spirit reign here—every winery has its own specialty and range of varietals, yielding a wide range of German-style wines as well as sparkling wines such as Iron Horse and Piper Sonoma, and of course all the usual reds and whites.

Some leading producers: Buena Vista (Sonoma), Dry Creek Vineyard (Healdsburg), Iron Horse (Sebastopol), Simi (Healdsburg).

Napa County. California's most famous—and certainly coolest—wine-growing district, the Napa River Valley lies between the Mayacamas Mountains to the west and the Vaca Mountains to the east. The reason for its international success may lie in the fact Napa very early on made developing high quality wines a priority. Non content to rest on its laurels, it continues still to pursue this policy. Then comes the homogeneity, relative but true, of Napa wines. Unlike in many neighboring wine-growing districts, here there is a distinct "Napa style," characterized by the predominance of Cabernet Sauvignon grapes (for reds) or Chardonnay (for whites). In this fairly deep valley, the best vineyards lie on the northeastern slopes, thereby benefiting from the morning sun but shaded from the blistering heat of the afternoon—conditions highly propitious to the firm, lively expression of the two main varietals. Just to the south of Sonoma and Napa is Los Carneros, a small district affected by the weather of San Francisco Bay, bringing markedly cooler temperatures than elsewhere in California. For this reason, many producers here have planted Burgundy varietals such as Chardonnay and Pinot Noir, which are yielding highly interesting still and sparkling wines.

Some leading producers: Caymus (Rutherford), Clos du Val (Napa), Diamond Creek Vineyards (Calistoga), Grgich Hills Cellar (Santa Helena), Inglenook (Rutherford), Mayacamas Vineyards (Napa), Robert Mondavi Winery (Oakville) Niebaum-Coppola (Rutherford), Stag's Leap (Napa) Beaulieu Vineyard (Napa), Newton (Santa Helena), Jo Phelps (Santa Helena).

Central Coast. This vast region covers an administrative area that includes vineyards located from San Francisco in the north to Santa Barbara in the south. Except for Lodi (east of San Francisco but benefiting from the cool climate of the river delta leading to the bay) and San Joaquin (very hot), all these vineyards lie close to the Pacific coast, which keeps temperatures relatively cool despite a great deal of sunshine in summer and fall. Although these regions do not enjoy the same reputation as those north of San Francisco, some of the California's best wineries are to be found in Santa Cruz and Livermore Valley, producing classic Cabernet Sauvignons and Chardonnays as well as wines from southern varietals such as Grenache, Syrah, and Barbera from Italy.

Some leading producers: Bonny Doon (Santa Cruz), Ridge Vineyards (Cupertino).

The Rest of the United States and Canada
California is not the only standard-bearer for American wine on the Pacific coast—the states of **Oregon** and **Washington** are also known for the quality of their wines. Developed much later than in California, rarely by local farmers, vinyards here reflected a desire to exploit cooler weather conditions in order to grow grapes from northern climes such as Burgundy (Pinot Noir and Chardonnay) and the Rhine Valley (Riesling, Gewürztraminer and Pinot Gris-Tokay).

Along with California, the cradle of American winemaking is to be found in the **Northeast**, along Lakes Erie and Ontario, and in Virginia. Even as Spanish monks were planting vines all around the Catholic missions they built as they moved north as far as San Francisco, English, German, Italian and French colonists also produced a good deal of wine from the eighteenth century onwards. There the resemblance stopped, however: whereas European vines can be transplanted to California without difficulty, all attempts to do the same thing in the east were doomed to failure, for a reason that would only be discovered in the second half of the nineteenth century. It turned out that phylloxera, a microscopic aphid, had lived in the United States since time immemorial, and although it did not attack local varieties, it had a field day when European rootstocks arrived.

Like the United States, **Canada** endured a period of prohibition between the two world wars. Since then, a state monopoly has governed the distribution of imported wines and spirits, without however seriously restricting the variety of foreign wines available. Local production remains highly limited, even though it has recently sought to boost its quality. **Ontario**'s vineyards, on the northern shore of Lake Erie not far from Niagara Falls, are noteworthy for their measures aimed at quality and for the rules of production observed voluntarily by their thirty or so wineries. Finally, in **British Colombia** a few vineyards are imitating the wines produced just across the border in the state of Washington, growing Riesling and Chardonnay grapes as well as hybrid varieties.

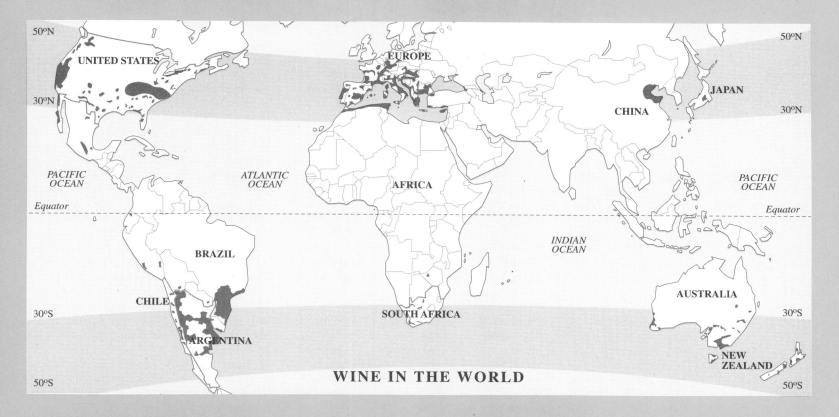

WINE IN THE WORLD

SOUTH AMERICA

Chile

Spanish missionaries, needing to make altar wine, planted the first vines in Chile back in the sixteenth century, generally of the Pais variety. In 1851, Silvestre Ochagavia imported good plants from France, realizing the potential of this isolated country where fruit grew easily in the shelter of the Andes. Today, only part of Chile's 116,000 hectares of vines are used to make quality wines—perhaps 20,000 hectares. The rest produce table grapes, ordinary wines, or *pisco*, the local brandy. Most of the high quality wines—supple, well-made, velvety and easy to drink—come from Cabernet Sauvignon and Merlot grapes (for reds) or Chardonnay, Sauvignon and sometimes Sémillon (for whites). There are three major wine-growing regions. Aconcagua, to the north, can be subdivided into two valleys, Aconcagua and Casablanca, the latter on the road to Valparaiso, making full, fat Chardonnays with aromas of pineapple and *chilimoya*. The central region includes the valleys of Maipo, Rapel, Curico, and Maule. The southern region, comprises the Itata and Bio-Bio Valleys. The finest vineyards are located principally in the central valleys, notably in Maipo around Santiago, which produces red wines with appealing aromas of eucalyptus and mint; Maipo is where old family firms such as Cousiño Macul and Concha y Toro make their top-quality wines (Antiguas Reservas and Don Melchior). This is where most French winemakers have come to develop great vintage wines, and many Chilean producers, alone or in joint ventures, increasin-

gly favor blends of varieties in order to rival the great wines, at prices far above to the local average.

Some leading producers: Don Melchior (Conca y Toro), Cousiño Macul (Penalolen), Los Vascos (Las Condes), Casa Lapostolle (Las Condes).

Argentina

Number one in South America with 211,000 hectares (500,000 acres) of vineyards yielding 12.6 million hectoliters of wine in 1996, Argentina is the fourth largest wine-producing country in the world. The first vineyard was planted in 1556 at Cuyo by a Jesuit priest using Criolla vines, a variety still widely grown today. Wine-growing subsequently developed thanks largely to the Italians, the Spanish and later the French who imported their own varieties. The vineyards lie at the same latitude as their Chilean counterparts on the other side of the Andes, but here the climate is quite different—more continental and more changeable. Although grapes are grown on a band one thousand miles long, the province of Mendoza supplies over 70% of the country's wine. South of Mendoza city, the Maipu and Lujan de Cuyo vineyards grow Cabernet Sauvignon and above all Malbec, a variety that is both supple and powerful, with hints of blackcurrant and spices. Tupungato has more success with Chardonnay, Gewürztraminer, Pinot Noir, and Merlot. San Juan province to the north, meanwhile, is hotter and accounts for 22% of the country's vineyards, while Salta, the northernmost province, grows grapes at an altitude of 5,500 feet, providing conditions perfectly suited to white grapes such as the extraverted, fiery

Torrontes. At the other end, Rio Negro is devoted above all to the production of sparkling wines, developed there by Moët & Chandon for nearly forty years. Investment is currently on the rise, as many winemakers from Bordeaux, Chile, America and Portugal realize the attraction of moving into this booming country.

AFRICA AND OCEANIA

North Africa

This region is one of the cradles of world viticulture, as the Carthaginians, followed by the Romans, grew vines here throughout antiquity. North Africa offers numerous attractions, beginning with its outstanding levels of sunshine. Vineyards are now cultivated along the coastlines of the three Maghreb countries, Tunisia (Bizerte, Tebourba, Grombalia, and Kelibia, all near Tunis), Algeria (Haut-Dhara and Medea near Algiers, Mascara and Tlemcen near Oran) and Morocco (Meknès, Casablanca, Oujda and Marrakesh). The precepts of the Islamic religion clearly limit the current development of wine-growing in the region.

South Africa

South Africa wine production began when Dutch traders on the maritime route to India imported vines to the Cape district in the mid-seventeenth century. These were planted in 1655 and the first grapes pressed on February 2, 1659. Vineyards spread from the tip of the cape inland, and now cover 106,000 hectares (250,000 acres), yielding 10 million hectoliters of wine. Given its isolation—the country was for many years subject to a boycott because of its system of apartheid—South Africa was not part of the revolution in New World wines. Quality is nevertheless improving and many changes have been introduced in the wine industry since 1994. Although the enormous KWW cooperative (with five thousand members) has long dominated the industry, an increasing number of independent estates are springing up. The wine-growing zone is divided into regions and districts. The Coastal Region includes the most prestigious districts: Constantia to the south of Cape Town, where the Mediterranean climate is ideal for Chardonnays, Sauvignons, and Rieslings as well as Constantia wine, a thick sweet wine made from Muscat of Alexandria; Stellenbosch, the country's wine-growing nerve center, which boasts the finest producers, notably of reds (Cabernet Sauvignon, Merlot, Syrah); and Paarl, thirty miles northeast of the Cape, home to KWW and many other quality cooperatives and estates. Breede River Valley, meanwhile, encompasses the districts of Worcester and Robertson, now undergoing major charges in quality. Finally, Elgin and the Walker Bay Region (Hermanus) benefit from a cooler, coastal climate which produces Chardonnays and Pinot Noirs to rival the wines of Burgundy.

New Zealand

Wine-growing was introduced into New Zealand in 1819 and owes its survival to a few individuals who defended and developed it, notably the Anglican missionary Samuel Marsden, the Scotsman James Busby, and French Bishop Pompallier. The vineyards have nearly disappeared on numerous occasions (there were just 179 hectares in 1923) owing to phylloxera and prohibition, which continued into the early 1980s. Today the industry breathes easier, with vineyards that have increased from 5,000 hectares in the early 1990s to 8,000 in 1996, yielding 573,000 hectoliters of wine in that year. The

vineyards are highly mechanized and maintain close links with the University of California at Davis, enabling producers to follow technical advances very closely. The vines belong to growers who sell their grapes to large firms controlling 90% of wine production.

A three-hour flight from Australia, New Zealand has seen its vineyards develop from north to south across its two islands, together some 1,000 miles long and appearing ideal for producing fruity, acidic wines from vines that appreciate cool weather. North Island, largely volcanic, is divided into several different zones: Auckland, Waikato/Bay of Plenty, Gisborne, Hawke's Bay, and Martinsborough/Wairapa/Wellington. South Island, which is more mountainous, has developed thanks to the country's most powerful producer, Montana, which acquired land in the Marlborough area in 1973. Apart from Chardonnay and Sauvignon—by far the most promising varieties—blends of Cabernet Sauvignon and Merlot also seem to work, as does Pinot Noir. A current trend is towards finding the best land, typically river beds strewn with fine pebbles.

Some leading producers: Cloudy Bay (Blenheim), Vidal (Hastings).

Australia

With 81,000 hectares (200,000 acres) of vines and 6.8 million hectoliters of wine in 1996, Australia appears as one of the most promising and exciting of New World producers, and is still a long way from revealing its full potential in terms both of soils and technology. The first vines were planted in Sydney by colonists in 1788, but Australian viticulture owes its true start to Captain John Macarthur at roughly the same period. Australia's wine-producing regions are located in the southeastern and southwestern parts of the continent. Apart from Tasmania (the island just south of Melbourne which produces Rieslings,

Chardonnays, Pinot Noirs and Cabernet Sauvignons) and Brisbane in eastern Queensland, the country may be divided into four major regions.

South Australia. The vineyards are located around Adelaide, to the south of the Flinders Range. Riverland produces the greatest volume, including Chardonnays at unbeatable prices. Barossa Valley was settled in the 1840s by Prussian families, whose influence can still be felt today. It is now home to Penfold's Grange. Clare Valley is cooler, more propitious to the Rhine's Riesling grape, which here takes on lemony aromas. Coonawarra is best known for its high-flying Cabernet Sauvignons grown in red earth that drains well. Eden Valley is another Riesling zone, yet is also home to Henschke Cellars' Syrah-based Hill of Grace wine. Adelaide Hills, a cool zone, has given birth to sparkling wines, Sauvignons, Chardonnays, and Merlots which are beginning to show their worth.

Western Australia represents only 2% of the country's output but includes some of its finest wines and greatest potential, notably in Margaret River, south of Perth, which enjoys conditions similar to Bordeaux. Chardonnay, Pinot Noir, Zinfandel, and Cabernet Sauvignon grapes are all particularly happy here.

Victoria is the most southerly region. Chandon in Yarra Valley makes sparkling wine, while Lindemans offers a Bin 65 Chardonnay. Liqueurs are also made from red Muscat and Muscadelle grapes.

New South Wales, to the northwest of Victoria, boasts dry Sémillons (Hunter Valley), long-maturing Chardonnays (Cowra) and fleshy Chardonnays and Cabernet Sauvignons (Mudgee).

Some leading producers: Chandon (Yountville), Henschke (Keyneton) Lindeman (Lindecombe), Penfold's (Auckland), Rockford (Tanunda) Petaluma (Crafers) Rosemount (Denman).

MAJOR VARIETIES

RED GRAPES

Cabernet Franc: This close relative of the Cabernet Sauvignon produces wines that are equally tannic but often less stiff in their youth. It is notably planted in Bordeaux, the Loire Valley, and many regions of South America.

Cabernet Sauvignon: This is the most famous variety of grape in the world. The wines made from it are high in color, markedly tannic, and long in the mouth. They convey aromas of red berries when young, maturing over time into a complex bouquet of cedar and tobacco. The great archetypal Cabernet Sauvignon wines come from Médoc, but the grape adapts well to almost all vine-growing latitudes.

Gamay: This variety from Beaujolais yields fruity wines with little tannin, except those that come from great vineyards such as Moulin à Vent, which age in a manner astonishingly similar to Burgundy's Pinot Noir.

Grenache: Able to produce wines that are not very structured but generously alcoholic even when providing high yields, Grenache too often does no more than that when grown in many southern vineyards. If less diluted, however, it displays fine tannins and smooth fullness, notably at Châteauneuf-du-Pape.

Malbec: A secondary variety in Bordeaux but the main grape in Cahors, Malbec has forged a remarkable reputation in South America, notably Argentina, where it has become one of the main vines. It produces straightforward wines with somewhat rustic tannins, but which can also display a great deal of finesse when made from modest yields.

Merlot: The other great Bordeaux variety, reigning in Saint-Emilion and Pomerol. But it has adapted to vineyards throughout the world, and the wines it produces—beginning with Pétrus, the most famous—are highly seductive thanks to a fleshy roundness and fruitiness that ages into woody scents with roasted overtones.

Mondeuse: This aromatic, tannic variety recalls Syrah, and is planted mainly in Savoy.

Mourvèdre: This highly original variety is used in Bandol, Provence, for great, tannic, powerful wines with a typically peppery aroma. Late ripening and a certain capriciousness have limited its spread.

Nebbiolo: A great variety from Piedmont, Nebbiolo produces wines that age long and well, combining firm tannins with marked acidity. Despite its great character, it ripens late and is generally limited to the Piedmont region.

Pinot Noir: The grape of red burgundies is one of the most capricious of all, and does not always manage to live up to its potential despite worldwide popularity. At its best, Pinot Noir produces extraordinary wines. Brilliant in color, they may attain dazzling aromatic finesse (blackcurrants, blackberry, redcurrant, with floral notes), remaining supremely elegant in the mouth without the massiveness of Cabernet Sauvignon or the thickness of Merlot, displaying perfect breeding and dynamism.

Sangiovese: The traditional variety in Tuscany, Sangiovese produces structured, fruity reds able to age well when yields are kept moderate. This is the main variety used in Chianti.

Syrah: These grapes are traditionally used in wines from the northern Rhône—Côte Rôtie, Hermitage, Cornas, etc. In recent years it has encountered increasing popularity outside Europe, notably in Australia where it is called **Shiraz**. It gives deep red wines that are fleshy, structured, and aromatic (blackcurrant and blackberry).

Tannat: This variety, high in tannin and color, is used mainly in Madiran, at the foot of the Pyrenees.

Tempranillo: The main grape grown in Rioja, Spain, Tempranillo makes wines that are complete, fleshy, and structured. It is currently being planted in a number of other counties.

Zinfandel: This variety is grown mainly in California, where it produces structured, straightforward wines that sometimes lack aromatic finesse.

WHITE GRAPES

Chardonnay: The most famous white grape in the world, this variety produces the great white burgundies. Easy to grow, Chardonnay adapts to almost any soil and climate, yielding fat, full wines with flavors ranging from hazelnuts to butter and even, in hotter climates, a taste of butter-candy.

Chenin Blanc: This variety is planted mainly in the Loire Valley and a number of New World vineyards where, alas, it is too often used to make ordinary white wines. At its best, that is to say in Vouvray and Anjou, it can give wines that are either very dry and fruity or, when the grapes are picked late, sweet wines of dazzling freshness and length in the mouth.

Furmint: This is the main grape used in Hungarian Tokay, and is at its best when attacked by noble rot. When this occurs, the individual berries on the bunch, called *aszu* grapes, must be picked one by one.

Gewürztraminer: This highly aromatic version of the Traminer grape produces fat, fragrant wines with aromas of roses and lichees.

Marsanne: Along with Roussane, this variety is used for great whites from the northern Rhône Valley (except Condrieu), notably Hermitage. Its wines are full, structured, and age admirably, though they sometimes remain discreet when young.

Muscat: This variety also exists as a table grape, and logically enough produces wines which taste just like that grape. In southern Europe, Muscat is often used to make fortified wines.

Pinot Blanc: This white-skinned version of the Pinot family is planted all across continental Europe. It yields wines that are well-balanced but—with few exceptions—fairly simple.

Pinot Gris: Also known in Alsace as Tokay (though unrelated to the region in Hungary), when planted in the right places this little-known grape can produce wonderful late-picked wines that age well. They are powerful enough to accompanying a dish of wildfowl.

Riesling: Along with Chardonnay, Riesling is certainly the greatest white varietal. And yet it is planted principally in Alsace, in Germany and other specific districts in continental Europe, leading many consumers to perceive it as a dry, fruity regional wine. In the best vineyards, this highly refined, svelte and elegant grape can make wines of aromatic complexity that are strikingly long in the mouth.

Sauvignon Blanc: Too often planted to make modest little wines, this variety produces a beverage that is the archetype of a lively white wine with aromas of flint, citrus fruit or boxwood. It is ideal for accompanying grilled fish and seafood, in Sancerre wines notably.

Silvaner: This predominantly German and Alsatian grape yields lively if simple wines.

Viognier: A highly aromatic variety, Viognier produces wines with a distinctive aroma of apricot. Planted at Condrieu in the Rhône Valley, it has recently become fashionable in many other hot, dry regions.

TECHNICAL GLOSSARY

Ampelography: The scientific study of vines and grapes.

Anthocyanins: Red pigments found in the skin and seeds of grapes, which give color to red and rosé wines.

Appellation: A regulatory system designed to define the origin and (in theory) quality of wine from a specific region. France was the first country to regulate production with its AOC label (*Appellation d'Origine Contrôlée*), followed by other European nations (DOC in Italy, DO in Spain, RD in Portugal, and so on).

Bleeding a vat: A vat is bled when the fermenting red must is allowed to run off prematurely. This technique is used, for example, in making rosé and pale wines.

Blending: After fermentation, wines from different grapes grown on the same estate may be blended to obtain different styles and qualities of wine from that vineyard.

Botrytis: During damp weather, a fungus called *Botrytis cinerea* can attack grapes on the vine, which will have unfortunate effects if a red wine is to be made, but may have entirely beneficial ones if it operates as the "noble rot" that produces sweet white wines.

Bud burst: The moment the when buds open and the first leaves appear. In the northern hemisphere this occurs in late March or early April, depending on geography and grape variety.

Cap: When red wine ferments, the solid matter (skins, seeds, and stems) forms a dense cap that floats on the surface of the liquid, pushed upward by the carbon dioxide generated during fermentation.

Carbonic maceration: A type of maceration used notably for making red wines to be drunk young. Whole bunches of grapes are placed in a vat pressurized with carbon dioxide, and the resulting maceration produces supple, aromatic wines naturally low in tannin.

Cask: Some wines are matured in casks of "new oak," that is to say barrels that have never been used before, which imparts a strong oak flavor. Wines matured in re-used casks produce a more subtle effect.

Chaptalization: The technique of adding sugar to the must. Every 17 additional grams of sugar per liter of must boosts the alcoholic strength of the wine by one percent.

Clone: A variety of vine produced in the lab from a single rootstock, so that every plant has the same genetic make-up.

Coarse: Refers to cloudy wine still undergoing fermentation, full of sugar and carbon dioxide, which can nevertheless be drunk young in autumn.

Cru: A wine made from specific vineyard with a recognized personality of its own. The vineyard may coincide with a single estate (in which case it is the same as a "château" in Bordeaux) or may be divided among several proprietors (as is the case in Burgundy). Sometimes translated as "growth," the term cru is usually employed in the various systems for ranking quality French wines: *grand cru*, *premier cru*, etc.

Crushing: Just prior to being placed in the fermenting vat, the grapes are lightly crushed (or, traditionally, trodden) to break the skin and force juice from the fruit.

Dessication (over-maturation): Bunches of grapes are sometimes allowed to dry out naturally, free from *Botrytis* (noble rot), producing a range of intense aromas that differ from those provoked by *Botrytis*.

De-stemming: The removal of stems and stalks from the grapes. If allowed to macerate in the must, they may give a grassy taste to the wine.

Disgorging: After champagne bottles have been slowly riddled and tilted, the sediment that has accumulated in the neck must be removed, or disgorged. Two methods exist: manual disgorging (the cap is simply removed, the sediment is automatically ejected by interior pressure, and the cap is immediately replaced), and cold disgorging (the bottle is first placed in an icy brine so that the sediment can be removed with no loss of wine).

Dosing: Once champagne has been disgorged, makers of sparkling wines add a small dose of sugary liqueur to add roundness to the final product. The relative sweetness of the dose will determine the style of champagne: 5 to 10 grams of sugar per liter will produce a "brut" champagne, whereas twice that amount will produce a "demi-sec." There is an art to correctly dosing champagne; it is often better to wait for a year after dosing so that the wine will have thoroughly assimilated the liqueur.

Drawing-off: A stage in winemaking, just prior to fermentation, that entails removing the deposits from the juice of white grapes

—these deposits (solid debris from the grapes, earth, and so on) might give the wine an unpleasant taste.

Fermentation, alcoholic: The transformation of sugars into ethyl alcohol, the alcoholic component of wine.

Fermentation, malolactic: The transformation of unstable malic acid into stable lactic acid. This process, sometimes called secondary fermentation, reduces the acidity of the wine and increases suppleness. It is beneficial to red wines and to certain whites that are subsequently aged in oak casks. It is undesirable, however, for dry whites that seek to retain all their freshness and aroma.

Filtration: A technique for clarifying wine by passing it through a filtering substance (earth, pad or membrane).

Fining: An operation that clarifies and stabilizes wine prior to bottling.

Fortified: Wines can be fortified during fermentation (thereby halting the process) by the addition either of alcohol (natural sweet wines) or sulfur dioxide (thick, sweet wines from Bordeaux and the Loire).

Free-run wine: As its name implies, this is the wine that runs out of the vat when the tap is opened. The matter remaining in the vat (skins, seeds and other solids) is then pressed, producing the darker press wine.

Grafting: When the phylloxera aphid invaded Europe in the late nineteenth century, local vines had to be grafted onto to American rootstocks to make them resistant to the parasite. The upper part of the resulting plant (stem, leaves, grapes) therefore remains the traditional *vitis vinifera* type whereas the American rootstock (usually given a name or number) is of another type.

Grape maturation (*véraison*): The moment when the grape berries on the vine begin to change color.

Hogshead (*barrique*): A barrel or cask that traditionally holds one-quarter the volume of a tun, therefore 63 U.S. gallons. A barrique in Bordeaux holds 228 liters, in Champagne 105 liters.

Kept on lees (*sur lie*): A method of aging wine without racking, so that the lees impart additional flavor to the wine.

Lees: The sediment, mostly composed of dead yeast cells, that accumulates at the bottom of vats, casks and bottles during fermentation. Since the lees may be a source of bacterial infection, most wines are racked several times prior to bottling. When it comes to some white wines, however, the lees contribute nitrogenous matter that enhances aroma.

Marc: The solid residue of grapes after the juice has been pressed (skin, seeds, stems, etc.).

Mildew (brown rot): A vine disease that appeared in France in the late nineteenth century, caused by a fungus that attacks the plant during rainy weather.

Must: The liquid obtained by pressing or crushing fresh grapes. European regulations stipulate that the alcoholic level of the juice has to remain below one percent. Must is therefore unfermented grape juice.

Noble rot: See Botrytis.

Non-grafted vine: Vines that have never been grafted onto a different rootstock.

Oidium: A vine disease caused by a fungal parasite originally from America. The fungus spreads over the leaves, from which it draws its sustenance. If unchecked, it can destroy an entire harvest; it is treated with sulfur.

Oxidation: The effect of air on certain components in wine (tannins, iron, sulfuric acid), which can modify the appearance and taste of wine. The maderization and aging of white wines are the result of oxidation.

Press wine: The dark, tannic wine produced by pressing the solid matter in the vat after the free-run wine has been drained.

Pressing out: An operation that involves separating the must (or wine) from the solid matter.

Pruning: Removing some of the growth of a vine in order to limit the number of bunches the plant will produce. Various pruning and training techniques yield differently shaped plants; in the classic "double Guyot" method, for example, only two branches are allowed

to develop, growing horizontally in opposite directions.

Pumping over: An operation that involves pumping wine from the bottom of the vat and spraying it over the top.

Punching the cap: An operation that involves pushing the cap down into the liquid must during fermentation, so that tannins and dark solid matter will enter into full contact with the wine.

Racking: Draining a wine from one recipient to another, in order to aerate it and remove the lees.

Riddling (*remuage*): When making sparkling wines, an operation that involves regularzly rotating a set of bottles placed on sloping boards riddled with holes so that the necks can be progressively tilted downwards, forcing the sediment toward the cap.

Rootstock: Following the phylloxera epidemic in the late nineteenth century, all European vines have been grafted onto resistant rootstocks, which come in a multitude of varieties.

Run off: A racking-type operation for red and rosé wines in which the liquid is freely drawn from the fermenting vat by gravity. It occurs after fermentation and signals the end of maceration.

Selective picking: When making thick, sweet wines from grapes with noble rot, picking is done in successive waves so that only perfectly botrytized grapes are selected. Not to be confused with the standard operation of sorting.

Sexual Confusion: A method of discouraging parasites—the vineyard is dotted with capsules containing the hormones of female butterflies, thereby exhausting males who attempt to mate fruitlessly. Reproduction of their parasitical offspring is thus limited.

Sorting: The operation of removing rotten or unripe grapes after picking but prior to fermentation. It applies to all wines and should not be confused with selective picking.

Stave-wood: The oak planks, split or sawn, used to make vats and casks.

Stem: The stalks that hold the grapes on the bunch will give a grassy taste to the wine if they are allowed to macerate with the must, which is why they are usually removed during de-stemming.

Thinning: A pruning operation that involves removing unwanted young growth from the vines.

Topping up: During aging, some wine will evaporate, so casks (or vats) must be regularly topped up in order to minimize contact with the air, which would trigger oxidation.

Tun: A traditional wooden recipient for wine, often made of oak, containing anywhere from 50 to 500 hectoliters. When used as a unit of measure, a "tun" originally held 252 U.S. gallons.

Varietal selection: Traditional selection of plants within a vineyard entailed the reproduction of the finest specimens found there, in an effort to increase quality all the while maintaining the diversity of the plant population. **Clonal selection**, in contrast, involves laboratory reproduction of a single specimen; all its offspring will be genetically identical.

Vine deformation (*coulure*): An abnormality in the appearance of vine stalks and leaves that indicates the presence of a viral infection.

Yeast: A fungus essential to all winemaking because it triggers the chain reaction called fermentation.
Natural yeast is found naturally on the winemaker's own property, as opposed to specially **selected yeasts** which may be added to the must for specific purposes (low-temperature fermentation, high alcoholic yield, and so on). When it comes to sparkling wines, additional yeast known as *levure de tirage* is added to the bottle in order to trigger the second fermentation that produces the bubbles.

TASTING GLOSSARY

Acescence: Excessive bacterial formation of acetic acid, producing the sour taste and smell of vinegar.

Acidity: An essential component of wine, contributing freshness to the overall balance. Excessive acidity will result in a biting, harsh taste, while insufficient acidity will yield a flabby wine. There are two types of acidity, stable and volatile. The most common stable acids are tartaric, malic, and citric acids.

Acidity, volatile: The dominant volatile (or fatty) acid is acetic acid. Volatile acidity is crucial to a wine's bouquet, and is only mentioned if excessive, because it will produce unpleasant aromas that rendered the wine commercially valueless.

Acidulous: Refers to a high level of acidity. Although bordering on the unpleasant, this quality may be acceptable in wines that strive primarily for freshness.

Aggressive: Said of wines in which excessive acid or tannins attack the taste-buds.

Alcohol: A key ingredient of wine produced by the fermentation of the sugar in grapes. Ethyl alcohol is the most important of the various alcohols found in wine. Measured in degrees (i.e., percentage by volume), alcohol brings warmth to wine, counteracting acidity.

Alcoholic: Said of wines with an excessive degree of alcohol.

Ample: Wine having a broad aromatic range and after-scents that fill the mouth fully and long.

Amylic: An aggressively acidulous taste suggesting varnish, bananas, or sour candy. It is due to an excess of amyl alcohol, generally produced by vinification at overly low temperatures.

Animal: A family of animal-type odors —venison, musk, leather. Formerly appreciated in old red wine, now often perceived as a defect.

Aroma: Strictly speaking, refers exclusively to the odors sensed by the rear nasal passage at the back of the palate. The term is widely used, however, for odors in general, and may also refer more specifically to smells directly derived from the grapes as opposed to smells produced by bottle-aging, these latter being known as the bouquet.

Aromatic: Indicates a high level of olfactory intensity triggered by wine made from grapes with naturally pronounced aromas.

Astringent: Marked by somewhat harsh tannins, making a wine feel dry on the gums. Acceptable for tannin-rich red wines which are expected to mellow; but there is a risk that the wine will dry with aging.

Austere: Lacking aroma, marked by acidity and/or tannins in the mouth. Typical of young wines.

Balance: When it comes to white wines, balance is based on acidity on the one hand, and alcohol and residual sugar on the other. For red wines, another factor is the level of tannins (the only factor that may change over time). Balance is a key concept in wine-tasting.

Balsamic: A family of odors evoking resin, incense, vanilla.

Bite: A high level of acidity that may be excessive or, in certain cases, attractive.

Bitter: One of the four sensations detected by the tastebuds (the others being sweet, sour, and salty). Distinct bitterness in a wine is due to coarse or excessive tannins.

Bouquet: The olfactory features perceived by the nostrils and rear nasal passage. Refers exclusively to the scents producing by bottle-agzing (called secondary or tertiary odors).

Cachet: A wine with "cachet" is one displaying originality and elegance.

Chaptalized: The perception of added sugar (during fermentation) which creates an imbalance between the fruit substance and alcoholic content.

Character: An overall impression made by a wine that displays an original personality.

Chewy: A wine with consistency and tannins, creating in the mouth the tactile impression of chewing.

Clear: A clean appearance devoid of particles, although for red wines it may suggest a lack of color. In the Champagne region, refers to wine before it becomes frothy.

Closed: A wine in a transitional state between its initial fruity aromas and its secondary mature ones. At this point, olfactory features are blocked by the predominant structure of acidity and tannins.

Cloudy: A muddy color which is normal during fermentation and maturation but highly abnormal in the bottle, suggesting that the wine is subject to a bacterial disease.

Coarse: An overall impression given by a heavy wine that lack finesse and character.

Color: The visual impression of a wine, in all its nuances. Color can be a good indicator of the effect of vinification methods and aging.

Corked: A moldy smell and taste produced by a poorly made or poorly handled cork.

Crisp: A pleasant, fruity level of acidity.

Delicate: A light, refined wine.

Dense: A wine made from highly concentrated fruit. May also refer metaphorically to impressions of smell and taste.

Distinguished: An elegant wine with a great deal of personality.

Dried-out: A wine which has lost its fruitiness and fatness, becoming overly acid or tannic.

Dry: When discussing still white wines, indicates the absence of perceptible residual sugars. For reds, suggests an astringency that may leave a dry sensation in the mouth (which then becomes a defect). When it comes to champagne, however, the French term for "dry" (*sec*) paradoxically means relatively sweet (in contrast to *brut*).

Dull: Lacking flavor due to abnormally low acidity.

Easy-to-drink: Synonymous with "smooth," refers to a supple, pleasant wine.

Fat: A measure of the richness and consistency of a wine, somewhere between fleshy and thick. Often synonymous with unctuous. More generally, refers to a pleasant rounded, supple, fleshy wine.

Feminine: Refers to a light, graceful wine.

Fired: A family of smells evoking smoky, grilled, roasted, or burned fragrances.

Firm: Refers simultaneously to the levels of acidity (higher than a lively wine) and tannins (lower than a harsh wine). Said of wines which have body and nerve.

Flat: A wine that has lost its olfactory qualities due to prolonged oxidation.

Fleshy: An impression of fullness and density in the mouth, created primarily by a wine's concentration, alcohol, and tannins.

Flinty: The mineral taste of flint found in some Sancerre and Chablis wines.

Floral: A family of scents evoking flowers such as acacia, hawthorn, peony, rose, violet and so on.

Foxy: A distinctive, cloying scent typical of indigenous American grapes, and detectable in certain hybrids varieties.

Fresh: Indicates a pleasant level of acidity, lending an impression of freshness in the mouth. Sometimes used to suggest that the wine has not aged.

Fruity: A family of scents including fresh fruit (red, black and other berries), nuts, and citrus fruit. Often misused to imply that the wine has retained an abundance of fruit flavors. Sometime used to suggest that the wine conveys the original flavor of the grapes.

Full: A wine which displays every key component and therefore fills the mouth. Such wines are obtained only by limiting the yield of the vines.

Full, very: A perfectly balanced, complete wine.

Full-bodied: A well-constituted wine (robust and fat) with marked alcoholic content.

Gamey: A perfume in the bouquet that suggests venison or other game.

Grassy: A special category of scents suggesting a lack of maturity in the grapes and/or stems.

Great: Refers to a great wine, well above average.

Green: A wine of somewhat excessive acidity, produced by insufficiently ripe grapes.

Hard: An excess of tannins and acidity. May soften over time.

Harmonious: A wine with well-balanced components that merge into a coherent whole.

Harsh: A wine dominated by excessive tannins.

Hazy: Indicates a lack of limpidness. Sometimes used figuratively to indicate a lack of aromatic crispness.

Heady: A wine rich in alcohol, almost to excess.

Hearty: A level of alcoholic intensity usually situated between warm and heady.

Heavy: A measure of the richness of a wine, most especially its consistency, which should be just short of viscous. Suggests a lack of acidity. Often used to refer to wines with high alcoholic content.

Honest: A straightforward wine without defects. Possesses all the basic qualities.

Insipid: A wine lacking aroma, acidity, and substance.

Lacking balance: Said of a wine in which one element dominates, such as acidity (in the mouth) or oakiness (in the nose).

Lactic acid: The acid obtained during malo-lactic fermentation. "Lactic" also refers to a family of scents derived from milk products (such as fresh butter), notably found in Chardonnays.

Lean: A wine lacking consistency and even substance.

Light: A balanced wine that is naturally low in alcohol, color and tannin.

Light-damaged: An abnormal taste that arises in certain wines, especially champagne, when over-exposed to light.

Limpid: A wine that is clean and clear in color, with no particles in suspension.

Lively: A wine with an acceptably high level of acidity, producing a light, fresh taste.

Long/length: The persistence, over time, of smells and tastes that linger in the mouth after tasting. A key feature of truly great wines.

Mellow: Round and well-matured.

Mercaptans: Sulfide compounds that create nauseating odors of sweat, garlic and even rotten eggs. Linked to a reductive process from insufficient aeration.

Moldy: An unpleasant taste provoked by poor conservation or rotten corks.

Mouth: The set of features perceived by the mouth, generally analyzed in terms of attack, mid-mouth and finish (or aftertaste).

Muscat: A scent typical of Muscat grapes.

Musky: A heavy, heady scent reminiscent of musk.

Oaky: A wine that has been fermented or aged in oak will take on aromas of vanilla, caramel or charcoal, depending on the extent to which the oak was charred.

Odor: Refers to the smell perceived directly by the nostrils, not to be confused with the aroma detected in the back of the palate.

Open: A balanced wine which has reached full maturity in the bottle. Its bouquet has attained maximum intensity and complexity, and its tannins have mellowed.

Pale: A wine with little color, almost translucent.

Pasty: A white wine with too much sugar and too little counterbalancing acidity. Leaves a thick, pasty aftertaste.

Persistent: Synonymous, if somewhat less specific, than "long in the mouth," referring to the perception of flavors and aromas after tasting.

Powerful: A generous, full wine high in alcoholic content, with a great deal of substance and olfactory intensity.

Rancio: A Spanish term suggesting a nutty, roasted flavor produced in certain wines by a long and slow oxidation (sherry, *vins jaunes*).

Rasping: Indicates a particularly high level of tannins.

Residual sugar: The sugar remaining after fermentation has transformed all the other sugar into alcohol.

Rich: A generous wine featuring numerous, well-balanced components.

Roast: When applied to wines made from botrytized grapes, describes the aroma produced by the final stage of complete withering or "roasting."

Robust: Intensely tannic, suggesting perhaps a slight temporary imbalance that nevertheless enables the wine to age well.

Rotten: A taste that may affect wines made from grapes stricken with gray rot. They lack aromatic cleanness and may even smell moldy.

Rough: Like the term harsh, indicates excessive tannins.

Rounded: An overall impression given by a smooth, supple wine (including non-aggressive tannins in red wine).

Sappy: Indicates a concentrated wine made from fine fruit substances.

Silky: A harmonious, smooth, elegant wine with low acidity.

Smoky: A special odor that evokes smoked foods. Often used to describe certain Sauvignons and Syrahs.

Smooth: Synonymous with "easy-to-drink," refers to a supple, pleasant wine.

Soft in the mouth: A smooth, supple wine with relatively little acid.

Solid: A well constituted, firmly built wine that usually requires aging.

Sour: Indicates a high degree of vinegar-like acidity.

Sour: The vinegary taste of wines suffering from acescence.

Spicy: A family of odors suggesting not only pepper but also cloves, juniper, nutmeg, and even parsley or chervil.

Stale: An overall impression that the wine is past its prime.

Stalky: If the grapes have not been destemmed before fermentation and the stalks are not ripe, they contribute a certain astringency to the wine.

Straightforward: An overall impression suggesting honest components free from defects or artifice, but not displaying any great quality.

Stripped: An old wine which has lost much of its substance.

Sturdy: A highly concentrated, well-structured wine that should age well.

Suave: A perfectly balanced wine in terms of sweetness and mellowness, with harmonious aromas.

Sugary: Sweetness which overpowers the other elements, usually due to a lack of acidity.

Supple: A wine with relatively low acidity.

Sweetish: A slight imbalance toward sweetness. Not as severe as sugary.

Syrupy: A highly concentrated wine, often low in acidity. Intended as a compliment when discussing rich, botrytized wines, otherwise has negative connotations.

Tannin: A substance found in the skin and seeds of grapes. A key component of red wines, its effect evolves over time.

Tartaric acid: One of the main stable acids in wine, although low temperatures sometimes trigger the precipitation of a harmless deposit of crystals called **tartrates**.

Thick: A general impression of a densely colored wine with great substance, heavy in the mouth. When discussing sweet white wines, "thick" or ("creamy") suggests a level of residual sugar somewhat inferior to a syrupy, botrytized wine.

Thin: A wine lacking structure and character.

Tile-red: A yellowish-red color acquired by red wines as they age.

Tired: Said of a wine that has temporarily lost its qualities, after being shipped, for example. The only solution is to let it rest.

Turbid: Like cloudy, indicates lack of clarity. Although normal during fermentation and maturation, it is abnormal in the bottle.

Unctuous: Generally speaking, refers to a fat and velvety sensation in the mouth. When it comes to sweet wines, indicates a rich, medium-sweet wine not quite as sugary as a syrupy one.

Vegetal: A family of odors that evoke vegetation rather than fruit (ferns, thyme, honeysuckle, mushrooms and so on) and are generally perceived as pleasant. Only a grassy scent is considered a defect.

Velvety: A fat, mellow wine rich in alcohol.

Warm: A richly alcoholic wine, though less rich than one that is heady.

Watery: Wine lacking concentration, made from grapes diluted by rain before or during picking.

Weak: An overall impression suggesting that the wine was made from weak components, usually due to watery grapes.

Well-matured: Refers to older wines in which the various components, especially tannins, have blended harmoniously.

Yeasty: Although yeast triggers all alcoholic fermentation, the term is generally not complimentary except when it refers to champagne or muscadet (both of which are kept on lees).

BIBLIOGRAPHY

Several thousand books have been written about wine, many of which provide wine lovers with valuable information. This author personally consulted a good number of them while writing this book, noting once again the wealth and variety of texts on wine, both past and present. Rather than an exhaustive bibliography designed for specialists, below is a limited range of books that are (relatively) easy to find and easy to read by all wine lovers, enabling them to extend, if not totally satisfy, their knowledge of the subject. In addition to books presenting an overview of the major subjects (history, vineyards, techniques, etc.), each section includes a title or two that develops a particular point in a lively way.

General

Lichine, Alexis. *The New Encyclopedia of Wines & Spirits.*

A new version of this delightful dictionary of wine by a major player on the twentieth-century wine scene, namely Alexis Lichine, a Franco-American wine trader and Bordeaux vineyard owner.

Le Larousse des Vins (Editions Larousse).

Stevenson, Tom. *Sotheby's World Wine Encyclopedia.*

Two serious, thorough encyclopedias.

Huet, Myriam. *Le Vin* (Editions de La Martinière).

A didactic and ingeniously illustrated approach to "learning about wine."

History

Dion, R. *Histoire de la Vigne et du Vin en France* (Flammarion).

Lachiver, Marcel. *Vins, Vignes et Vignerons* (Libraire Arthème Faillard).

Two accurate and well-documented histories of wine in France.

Johnson, Hugh. *The Story of Wine* (Mitchell Beazley, 1998).

A remarkably written, magistral book teeming with anecdotes.

Pijassou, Robert. *Un Grand Vignoble de Qualité: Le Médoc.*

Written in 1980, and based on a doctoral dissertation, this is the most complete and fascinating monograph on a famous wine-growing region. Unfortunately out of print and hard to find.

Ginestet, Bernard. *Thomas Jefferson à Bordeaux* (Mollat).

A delightful exegesis of the travel diary of a late eighteenth-century wine-loving visitor to Bordeaux, future American president Thomas Jefferson.

Vineyards around the World

Johnson, Hugh. *World Atlas of Wine* (Simon & Schuster, 1994).

For thirty years now, the most complete wine atlas available.

Bazin, Jean-François, Pierre Casamayor and Michel Dovaz. *L'Or du Vin* (Hachette).

The most costly wines in the world.

Les Grands Vins du Monde (Hatier).

Cobbold, David. *The Great Wines and Vintages* (Chartwell Press, 1997).

The world's most famous wines.

Steinberg, Edward, *The Making of a Great Wine: Gaja and Sori San Lorenzo* (Ecco Press, 1996).

A day-to-day account of Angelo Gaja's famous vineyard in Piedmont.

French Vineyards

Ginestet, Bernard (ed). *Le Grand Bernard des Vins de France* (Editions Jacques Legrand).

Over twenty volumes, each one devoted to a major vintage.

Atlas des Vins de France (Hachette).

Féret. *Bordeaux et ses Vins.*

This annotated list of all the Bordeaux vintages is now an institution.

Broadbent, Michael. *Wine Vintages* (Antique Collectors Club, 1997).

Three centuries of tasting notes!

Renvoisé, Jacques. *Le Vin, Art ou Bluff?* (Editions du Rouergue).

An interesting and well-founded, if polemical, viewpoint on wine, vinification and wine-growers.

Doutrelant, Jean-Marie. *Les Bons Vins et les Autres* (Points Seuil).

The same theme as the preceding book, but written twenty years earlier and with a dash of humor.

Grape Varieties

Robinson, Jancis. *Guide to Wine Grapes* (Oxford University Press, 1996).

A thorough and readable presentation of the world's major grape varieties and the wines they yield.

Vinification

Chaptal, Jean-Antoine. *L'Art de Faire le Vin* (Editions Jeanne Laffitte).

A key—and fascinating—treatise that laid the foundations of modern oenology.

Peynaud, Emile. *Le Vin et les Jours* (Dunod).

The lessons of half a century of work by Bordeaux's greatest oenologist.

Halliday, James (with Hugh Johnson). *The Vintner's Art/How Great Wines are Made* (Simon & Schuster, 1992).

A technical and detailed description of vinification methods throughout the world.

Wine Tasting, Food and Wine

Puisais, Jacques. *Le Goût Juste* (Robert Laffont).

Bourgignon, Philippe. *L'Accord Parfait* (Editions du Chêne).

Two books on matching wine and food perfectly.

Montignac, Michel. *Boire du Vin pour Rester en Bonne Santé* (Flammarion).

A complete overview of medical research into the beneficial effects of wine on health.

I N D E X

PHOTOS CREDITS

ACKNOWLEDGMENTS

The author would like to thank all the wine-growers, traders, oenologists, cellar masters, vineyard foremen, merchants, and sommeliers as well as all the great wine connoisseurs who have fueled his knowledge and enthusiasm for wine over the years. Without them—and without the wine they produce, sell and taste—writing this book would have been a vain undertaking.

He would also like to thank *La Revue du Vin de France* and its editorial staff, with whom he has worked over the past decade in digging up fine wines and discovering vineyards. Among the magazine's team, special mention goes to Michel Betane and Michel Dovaz, who agreed to read the manuscript in a critical yet constructive spirit.

Thanks are also due to Mathilde Hulot and Pascale Cassagne for their help in producing the book, notably the Connoisseur's Guide, as well as to Sophie Guemès for permission to borrow several quotations from writers and poets included her anthology *Le Vin et l'Encre* (Editions Mollat).

Finally, the author is grateful to Ghislaine Bavoillot and her staff at Flammarion for the enthusiasm and professionalism they displayed throughout the making of *The Book of Wine*.

The publisher would like to extend heartfelt thanks to Jean-Paul Kauffmann, who appreciated the idea behind the book right from the start and made it possible to convince author Thierry Desseauve to undertake this long-term task.

The publisher also thanks Caves Augés and its sommelier, Marc Sibar, for the warm welcome and valuable information they provided. Lydia Elhadad, finally, who organized the "Théâtre des Sens" exhibition for the Colbert Committee at the Palais de la Découverte (May 15, 1998 to January 3, 1999), kindly authorized us to use certain quotations from the exhibition (captions on pages 7, 117, and 181).

Editorial Direction
GHISLAINE BAVOILLOT
SUZANNE TISE-ISORÉ

Editorial Coordination
SANDRINE BALIHAUT MARTIN

Translation
DEKE DUSINBERRE

Copy-editing
BARBARA MELLOR

Design
MARC WALTER-Bela Vista

Production
MURIELLE VAUX

Printed and bound by Canale, Italy

© Flammarion 1999
ISBN: 2-08013-662-3
Numéro d'édition: FA 3662
Dépôt légal: October 1999